INTERFACE DESIGN

with Photoshop

J. Scott Hamlin

New Riders

New Riders Publishing, Indianapolis, Indiana

Interface Design with Photoshop

By J. Scott Hamlin

Published by:
New Riders Publishing
201 West 103rd Street
Indianapolis, IN 46290 USA

Copyright © 1996 by New Riders Publishing

Printed in the United States of America 1 2 3 4 5 6 7 8 9 0

This book was produced digitally by Macmillan Computer Publishing and manufactured using 100% computer-to-plate technology (filmless process), by Shepard Poorman Communications Corporation, Indianapolis, Indiana.

Library of Congress Cataloging-in-Publication Data

```
Hamlin, J. Scott
     Interface Design with Photoshop/Scott Hamlin.
        p.  cm.
     Includes index.
     ISBN 1-56205-668-9
     1. Computer graphics. 2. Adobe Photoshop.
  3. Computer interfaces. I. Title.
  T385.H32953 1996
  006.6'869--DC20                          96-42372
                                              CIP
```

Warning and Disclaimer

Publisher	*Don Fowley*
Publishing Manager	*David Dwyer*
Marketing Manager	*Mary Foote*
Managing Editor	*Carla Hall*

Acquisitions Editor
Steve Weiss

Senior Editor
Sarah Kearns

Development Editor
Laura Frey

Project Editor
Karen Walsh

Copy Editors
Gina Brown
Jennifer Eberhardt
Larry Frey
Charles Gose
Howard Jones

Technical Editors
Nathan Clement
Kim Scott

Associate Marketing Manager
Tamara Apple

Acquisitions Coordinator
Stacey Beheler

Administrative Coordinator
Karen Opal

Cover Designer
Aren Howell

Production Manager
Kelly D. Dobbs

Production Team Supervisor
Laurie Casey

Graphics Image Specialists
Steve Adams
Debi Bolhuis
Kevin Cliburn
Dan Harris

Production Analysts
Jason Hand
Bobbi Satterfield

Production Team
Daniel Caparo
Joe Millay
Scott Tullis
Megan Wade
Christy Wagner

Indexer
Rebecca Hornyak

About the Author

J. Scott Hamlin is a graphic designer/writer who specializes in developing computer graphic illustration techniques. He has written for a variety of periodicals in the computer graphics industry including *Computer Artist* and *PC Graphics & Video*. Scott is the co-author of *CorelDRAW! Design Workshop* by Sybex Publishing and is a former art director.

After spending long hours staring at cathode ray tubes, Scott's #1 hobby is playing with his two children, Aidan and Audrey, for as long as they'll put up with him. He also enjoys paper engineering and playing the guitar and keyboard. Scott has also been known to sneak away for a game of volleyball and a little jet skiing from time to time.

Dedication

In memory of our family beach house on Balboa Island which was sold along with the closing of my Grandmother's estate during the production of this book. My grandparents, Herb and Jean Runner, bought a house that was little more than a shack that became the focal point of some of the most wonderful memories of my and my family's lives. Some of my best inspirations came to me while observing the beauty of Balboa Bay, and the memory of seeing my son and niece play where my sister and I once played will inspire me for years to come.

Acknowledgments

I am unable to thank my wife, Staci Hamlin, enough for her support, encouragement, and long-suffering attitude. Without her I wouldn't have been able to write a single word of this book. She is such a profound blessing to me that I cannot help but be continually humbled. I am also deeply grateful for my children, Aidan and Audrey, who offered welcome relief from the unrelenting bombardment from those cathode ray tubes. I couldn't have made it through some of the later chapters without playing with my little boy in the evenings at the pool (not to mention our weekend at Disneyland) and my little girl's first laughs gave me a boost that carried me through the final days of production.

I can't thank Steve and Judy Penn enough for providing me with an office within their home. Their support over the years has been instrumental in the development of my skills and my career. I would also like to thank Steve and his co-workers at Applied Science Fiction for providing valuable technical information ranging from how to install that pesky Windows NT to the finer points of a pixel.

It was a pleasure to work with the team at New Riders: Laura Frey, Stacey Beheler, Jennifer Eberhardt, Karen Walsh, Steve Weiss, and David Dwyer were all as helpful and supportive as they were professional. Their dedication to producing high-quality products have made this book much more worth the price you've paid for it. I'd especially like to thank Laura for putting up with my near daily rantings and David for bearing with me while we had a baby, moved into a new house, and quit my art director position before I started on this book.

I want to thank Cindy Taylor at Human Code for getting me together with Kyle Anderson and David Avila and their excellent work as well as the work of the near legendary Chipp Walters. Part of the inspiration for this book came from observing the depth of talent at Human Code and CDFactory. Thanks, also, to Brad Johnson, Danny Johnson, Brandee Selck, Tom Messina, Mike Cadunzi, Frank Wanicka, Nancy Tweddell, Bob Hone, Maria Marchetti, Todd Reamon and Rick Ligas who all contributed their excellent work to the Gallery of Real-World Images.

My thanks to Tony Jones at Sun Dog Limited for his contribution and willingness to step in a little late in the game. Also, I'd like to thank Teri Campbell at Fractal Design for taking time from her busy schedule to help me find Tony.

I apologize if I've forgotten anyone. Authors apparently always write these things late at night just as the publisher's about to unleash some big strong ape-looking guy to break our legs (Laura Frey says they never break your fingers because you've still gotta be able to type) if you don't turn the rest of the pages on time.

It is only by the grace of God that I came to be capable of doing this book. It is my hope that He be glorified by it since it is by His strength and grace that I was able to produce it.

Trademark Acknowledgments

All terms mentioned in this book that are known to be trademarks or service marks have been appropriately capitalized. New Riders Publishing cannot attest to the accuracy of this information. Use of a term in this book should not be regarded as affecting the validity of any trademark or service mark. Photoshop is a registered trademark of Adobe, Inc.

Contents at a Glance

Table of Contents

Part III   Extras

Introduction

Ever since mankind began creating devices that made life easier, we have been faced with the problem of generating effective ways for human operators to interact with and utilize these gizmos. Often the interface to these time- or energy-saving wonders was so difficult to interact with that many users returned to their old methods. Although some complex interface paradigms have become universally accepted and used, such as QWERTY touch typing system on typewriters and computer keyboards, most segments of the market continually strive for more and more user-friendly interface paradigms. As multimedia and web mediums have advanced, developers have been plagued with the same challenge: to create an interface that aids the user's experience in the virtual realm rather than one that hinders it.

Photoshop has played a central role in multimedia and web graphic design as both mediums have developed into mass markets, particularly in the area of interface design. The complete control over bitmap images that Photoshop provides has made it the natural processing center for multimedia and web imagery. Although Photoshop does not manipulate mediums that have glamorized multimedia and the web such as video, animation, and sound, the still image is nevertheless the backbone of new media design. Interfaces, buttons, props, and other static images provide the framework for users to navigate and experience multimedia and an ever-increasing number of web sites.

Recent advances in intuitiveness and power are making it more and more feasible for these tasks to be performed by only one or two individuals. Just as the advent of desktop publishing forced layout artists to become graphic designers and writers to become prepress experts, the overwhelming growth of the web and multimedia is forcing programmers, sound editors, and webmasters to become interface designers to remain competitive.

A series of important, and sometimes complex, factors are involved in generating successful multimedia titles and web sites. For multimedia, interface designers often must work with (or be) writers, programmers, producers, project managers, videographers, sound engineers, and 2D and 3D animators. For web site development, interface designers often must work with (or be) writers, programmers, and webmasters. Both mediums have advantages that the interface designer can exploit and limitations that the designer must avoid, as you will see in Chapter 1.

Assumptions

This book assumes that you have a working knowledge of Adobe Photoshop. Although a strong effort has been made to provide thorough step-by-step instructions, most basics of Photoshop are not covered in this book. Although this book mentions the use of other applications, such as CorelDRAW! and Ray Dream Studio, their coverage is largely limited to how they relate to interface design with Photoshop. Similarly, although HTML, CGI, Java, and Lingo coding are often critical for implementing multimedia, there is no discussion of these topics in this book. This book focuses on the role of the interface designer as it relates to Adobe Photoshop.

How This Book Works

This book covers many of the skills and techniques that an interface designer needs to create an intuitive and inviting interface. Although this book has a general flow from basic to more advanced topics, an effort has been made to make each chapter self-contained so that you will not have to start from the beginning for the latter chapters to make sense. Chapters 1–6 can be viewed as basics and Chapters 7–13 can be seen as more advanced and specialized topics. The Gallery of Real-World Images demonstrates many of the techniques covered in this book in action and features some of the leading interface designers in the industry. Appendix A offers you some general Photoshop tips, and Appendix B discusses plug-ins to deliver multimedia over the web.

PART I

Basic Interface Design

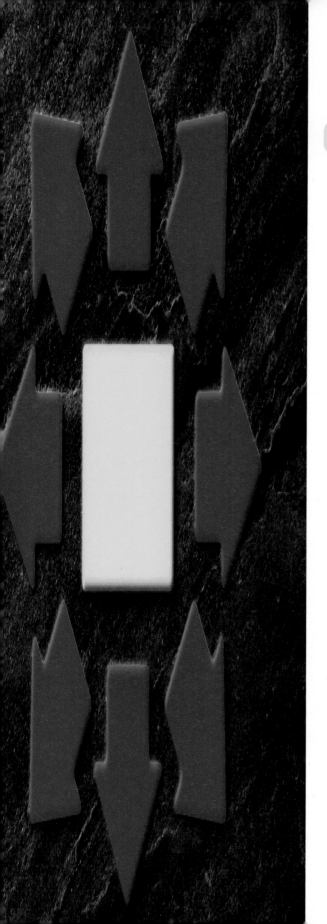

CHAPTER 1

Interface Design

Interfaces must conform to the particular nuances of their users: human beings. Most interfaces are dependent on modes of operation established by real world interface elements that include everything from a light switch to a typewriter. These modes of operation can be referred to as elements of interface design and are often grouped into patterns of structural and navigational methodology that can be referred to as paradigms. It is often much easier to embark on the interface design process with a general understanding of common elements of interface design and common paradigms.

Covered in this chapter:

► Common Interface Design Elements

► Establishing Structural Metaphors and Conventions

► Architectural Considerations

► The Sketch

Common Interface Design Elements

Each component of an interface serves a purpose whether it's the background, a button, or a video screen. Using these elements effectively can mean the difference between whether or not a multimedia title or web page is enjoyable and successful at getting the message across. The following list is not comprehensive; rather it represents those areas that provide the interface designer with the most control over how well-received the title or web page will be.

- ► The Background

- ► Buttons

- ► VHS-Type Controls

- ► Sliders

- ► Pop-Up Menus

- ► Video Screens

- ► Cursors

The Background

Textured backgrounds are used to provide attractive backdrops for various media (see fig. 1.1). Typically, backgrounds are tiled on web pages. A background can be used as a visual cue for users by applying a different background for different sections of a project. Backgrounds should not be so vibrant or wild that they distract from the main content. Usually the goal is to generate a background that supports the theme of the project without calling undue attention to itself.

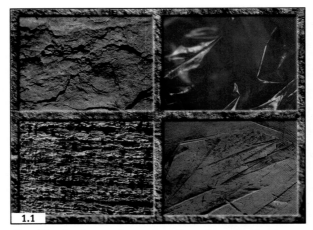

Attractive backgrounds, such as these from the Corel Professional Photo CD-ROM collection, can serve as the foundation for many multimedia titles.

Buttons

Buttons come in just about any shape and size a designer can imagine (see fig. 1.2). Buttons can be pictures, design elements, digital video, or 2D or 3D animations. Buttons can be made up of two images: what the button looks like in its normal state and what the button looks like when it is in its depressed state. These states are commonly referred to as *up* and *down states*.

Buttons shouldn't be so small that a user has difficulty finding them or clicking on them. On the other hand, buttons shouldn't be so large that they call excessive attention to themselves. Like backgrounds, avoid colors and textures on buttons that overly distract the user from the main content.

1.2

Buttons come in all shapes and sizes. Anything on the screen can serve as a button, but it helps to set apart the button in some way to help the user determine which items on the screen are clickable.

VHS-Type Controls

Digital videos, animations, and linear presentations often use VHS-type controls—just like a VCR. Typically these include controls for going forward, backward, pausing, stopping, going to the beginning, and going to the end (see fig. 1.3).

These controls should be created at a logical size. When the video is the most important aspect of the project, the controls can logically be bigger. If the video is just one part of many content vehicles such as text fields, still images, audio, and animation, the video controls should be more in line with the other controls.

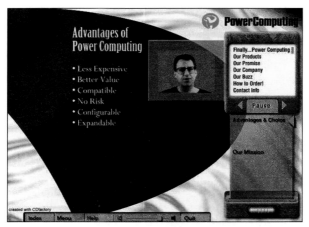

1.3

This interface created by CD Factory features VHS-type controls for a video screen that slides underneath the menu panel when not being used. The index, menu, help, volume, and quit controls can be hidden with a click of a button.

Sliders

Sliders are interactive controls the user can click on and slide to the desired option. Sliders are commonly used to navigate maps and flowcharts, as well as points of a project that provide users with multiple options (see fig. 1.4). Sliders can also be used to control volume, speed, and other variable controls. See Chapter 13, "Sliders, Dials, Switches, Doodads, and Widgets," for more on sliders and related controls.

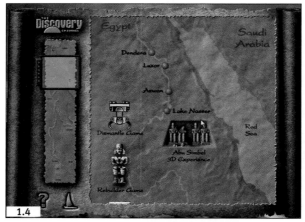

1.4

This innovative slider developed by Human Code for Discovery Channel Multimedia enables users to scroll up and down a miniature map that corresponds to parts of a larger map. The user can then click on various points on the larger map to jump to those points.

Pop-Up Menus

Pop-up menus can be designed to appear when a user clicks on a button or predefined area; pop-up menus enable designers to provide additional functionality to the interface without cluttering the screen. Designers can also have part of the interface scroll away to reveal menu options underneath, as shown in fig 1.3. Work pop-up or scroll-away menus into the theme and interface whenever possible. Because they are among the more mundane aspects of a project, pop-up menus should obstruct as little of the interface as possible when they are displayed.

Video Screens

Most computers are incapable of displaying full-screen video. For those computers that are capable, however, video and accompanying sound take up so much memory that these options are often used sparingly. Thus a video screen can be built into interfaces that utilize digital video or animation. If video is not the main driving element of the project, the interface designer should consider creating a retractable video screen. The retractable video screen will provide more space on the screen for other elements when no video is playing.

Cursors

Many authoring programs enable users to use images, video, and animations as cursors. Cursors can be used in conjunction with rollover events to provide users with visual cues and navigational controls. Often, cursors are kept between 1–4 bits so that they load and display quickly.

Establishing Structural Metaphors and Conventions

Guiding principles exist to serve as parameters for the interface designer. All design rules are devised to be broken, but the structural metaphors, conventions, and related principles can act as focal points for the initial design phase. The objective is rarely to completely befuddle the user as he attempts to navigate virtual worlds. In most cases, the interface designer's job is to create a navigational scheme and paradigm that are intuitive and inviting. Keeping the following ideals in mind while designing an interface can help make the user's experience more rewarding and your title or site more successful.

Using Established Metaphors

You can design established metaphors for your interface so that the user's learning curve is not so extreme. When a user sees an exit sign, for example, he has a good idea that the sign means he should exit or quit. The user will most likely be able to recognize that a light switch signifies on and off, that a turtle and a bunny mean slow and fast, and that a doorway leads to another area. Interfaces also can be based on an overall metaphor, such as a television set, an airplane cockpit, or a computer terminal. An interface that is based on an established metaphor often requires less guesswork for the user. Interface designers can also take advantage of established paradigms in user-interfaces of the platforms on which the titles or web pages are viewed—Windows 95 and the Mac OS, for example. Most Windows and Mac OS users, for instance, know that they can click on the buttons in the upper right corner of their application to minimize and maximize the application.

Transparency, Intuitiveness, and Style

In your interfaces, you should strive to achieve a balance between the desire for style and the need for intuitiveness or usability. The attractiveness of your interface will not matter if the typical user cannot determine how to navigate it. In general, resist the urge to overwhelm the user with excessive stylistic elements, but don't restrain yourself to the point of creating a dull interface. Many users won't waste time waiting for large downloads of material that have nothing to do with matter at hand, and yet if you fail to capture the user's interest, he won't hesitate to find another, more exciting place to explore.

Often the key to establishing a balance between transparency, intuitiveness, and style is found by analyzing the role of the interface in the presentation. Subject matter and the intended audience often provide the defining balance between transparency and style. If the interface metaphor is part of the experience then the style can be a little more pronounced. If the interface lacks a driving theme and is just the vehicle for relaying the information, then the style should probably be reigned in. For example, a multimedia title that uses a spaceship panel as its interface metaphor can probably afford a little more stylistic latitude than a corporate web site for a conservative company. A series of psychedelic-colored buttons that play a clip from a popular hard rock band might be out of place in a title about wine-tasting stops in the Napa Valley. These buttons would be, however, perfectly appropriate on a title featuring popular hard rock lead guitarists. A wild interface may not be distracting if the content is itself boisterous.

The main idea is that the interface should be as transparent as possible to the user to maximize the impact of the actual content. This principle is often referred to as *transparency*. The user should be able to see through the interface to get to the purpose of the multimedia title or web site. The interface design should not affect the user's ability to receive the information. If users are not distracted or confused by the interface, they will receive the information or message without inhibition.

Transparency is not always wholly ideal. Web sites, for example, often rely on navigational elements for their graphic appeal. Also, some markets expect a certain level of the "wow" factor. The high-tech industry, for instance, is coming to expect more designed atmospheres in the virtual realms it reviews. With potential clientele being bombarded with media, titles and web pages are forced to become more and more seductive, and the interface design is being called on to be as appealing as it is functional.

Less Is Best (Especially on the Web)

It is amazing how easy it is to overwhelm a user within 640×480 pixels. Too many buttons or a paradigm that is difficult to decipher can result in a user giving up on a title or web site prematurely. Typically it is unnecessary to display all available options and buttons on the screen at one time. Controls that are not used often such as Help and Quit can be tucked away in a pop-up menu or a dialog box, similar functions can be grouped, and features for advanced users can be given keystrokes. For web sites, this "less is best" principle is particularly important because download times are a major driving factor as to what is and is not feasible on web pages. For both multimedia and the web, the interface designer should strive to keep the interface as simple and digestible as possible while providing as much user-friendly functionality as possible.

Size

An interface designer is constantly faced with the need to balance the size of the interface elements with the size of the area where the main content will be viewed. A button that is too small may be easy to overlook, whereas a button that is too big can draw too much attention to itself and take away from the content. This does not mean that the interface should be as small as possible. If a multimedia title is based largely on digital video, the interface may need to take up more space because digital video is typically small due to limitation of the CD's storage capacity and the performance limitations of the typical computer.

Each element within an interface should be no bigger than it needs to be and no smaller than it has to be. A video screen doesn't need to be much larger than the size of the actual video, but it has to be at least as big as the video it will be displaying. All the elements of the interface must be integrated on the screen, but not all are equally important. A button that will be used constantly throughout the title or site is a good candidate for being oversized. Buttons that are not likely to be used often can be smaller, but not so small that they are difficult to click on.

Consistent Placement

One quick way to lose users is to keep them guessing about where they can find important functions. If the Exit button is in the upper left corner on one screen and the lower-right on another, users will likely become confused and frustrated and possibly leave the site. A successful paradigm enables users to learn something once and then be able to use that knowledge throughout the title or web site. After users learn the position and function of a button, they will likely assume that it will perform the same function as a button in the same position in another section.

A consistent metaphor can be used in lieu of consistent placement. For example, users can learn to click on the screen of various makes and models of antique televisions to view a video, even if the video screens are not positioned in the same place. Users can learn to associate a function with a color or sound as well. However, color-based and sound-based metaphors may not be effective for color-blind or hearing-impaired individuals.

Using Color

Strategic use of color can help guide users through an interface as well as assist in generating the tone of the paradigm. Interfaces can have attractive textures that utilize a limited palette of colors. In most cases, a neon or solarized interface would likely call too much attention to itself, whereas a more muted yet attractive interface may provide the appropriate balance. Often, browns and grays (or neutral colors) are good because they provide nice contrast for more colorful images in the foreground. Again, color usage may be determined by the subject matter. If the subject matter is about the colors of the rainbow, for example, you need to create an overall colorful interface.

Using Sound

Effective use of sound can help guide users through an interface. If a user has learned that he will hear a cowbell after he clicks on button A and a fog horn after he clicks on button B, he will be clued into the fact that the cowbell sound means he has clicked on the wrong place if he needed to click on button B. Soundtracks for projects with multiple themes also help the user navigate a title or site. For example, if the user becomes used to hearing a classical piano while in one theme, he will instantly know that he is in a new theme when he hears a different soundtrack. Whereas the imagery will often provide visual confirmation for these events, sound adds a level of verification that makes the interface subtly more intuitive. Sounds can also be used with rollover events, discussed in the next section.

Cursors and Rollover Events

Cursors within an interface can provide valuable visual cues for users. Many authoring programs enable developers to bring about events when a user rolls a mouse over a defined area—even if the user doesn't click within the area. These events are referred to as *rollover events*. For example, the cursor can be designed to display a miniature exit sign when the user rolls the mouse pointer over the exit button or the sound of rushing water can be designed to play when the user rolls over buttons that take the user to a discussion on the Amazon.

Rollover events are also useful for providing hints and adding functionality. For instance, a small tag can be made to pop up when the user rolls over a button whose purpose may not be clear or a pop-up menu can be made to display more options associated with a given element in the interface.

Icons versus Radio Buttons

Users usually need some visual indication of what a button does. Buttons can have text or icons on them, or text or icons to the side or underneath them. One disadvantage of a button with text on it (also known as a radio button) is that you limit your title or web site to a particular language, thereby alienating those users who do not understand it.

One way to avoid the use of text (and avoid the alienation of users) is to create icons or symbols that are universally interpretable. This, however, can be difficult and dangerous. For example, you might think that a button that depicts a tree for the exit button (as in "make like a tree and leave") is clever, but this will almost certainly confuse many users. In addition, symbols do not have the same universal meaning among different cultures. A hand gesture that means enter in one culture may mean have a crude meaning in another. Effective visual icons are often difficult to generate.

If you have the room, some of your buttons can have both text and an icon on the button. Another solution might be to create a rollover event for the button so that if the mouse lingers over the button, a pop-up text flag indicates the button's function.

Architectural Considerations

An interface is largely subject to the structure of the multimedia title or web site. A series of buttons may make sense in one architectural approach but not in another. And an interface metaphor may not fit with one paradigm but be perfect for another. Many established and common architectures exist.

Architectures can be effectively mapped out and storyboarded with flowcharts. Flowcharts and storyboards are extremely valuable tools for interface designers because they allow for the design of the interfaces to be made with the entire project in mind—allowing for continuity in the interfaces. Also, if one interface is going to be used globally, designers can plan for the needed functionality within the entire project and devise accordingly.

Linear/Multilinear

A linear structure is the most basic and, perhaps, boring architecture (see fig. 1.5). Interactive presentations, whether on the web or within a multimedia title, are as easy for most users to grasp as they are for most users to lose interest in. Linear structures are useful for content directed at children or for portions of a project that require a series of screens to convey the message. Web sites that are geared toward conveying a focused message use this structure effectively.

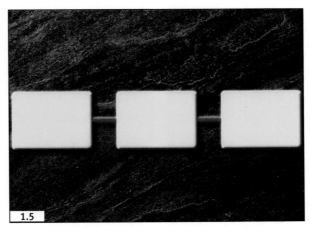

1.5

Linear paradigms are as intuitive as they are dull.

A variety of methods exist for making a linear architecture interesting. Multimedia titles utilize local interaction with various elements on-screen to liven up each area. With this method, the user clicks on an image, and a brief animation, sound effect, or other element results. A video screen, soundtrack, and narrator can also help make the linear experience less tiresome. Another method that can be used is making the project multilinear. Depending on choices the user makes, the project can be made to branch apart at certain key points so that the user is given multiple variations to experience.

Linear structures typically utilize controls similar to those found on a VHS player. Assuming the project can be self-running, controls for going forward, going backward, pausing, stopping, going to the beginning, and going to the end are common. A map of the entire path can be handy for users who do not have time to view the entire storyline. With a map, users can jump to the point where they left off or skip areas they are familiar with.

Hierarchy

A hierarchical structure is the most common structure used in many web sites and a large number of multimedia titles. A main screen that branches out to various areas drives this architecture. This paradigm can be made to go as many levels as desired from the original screen by building a series of submenu screens. Caution must be taken, however, to prevent your users from getting lost. Anyone who has surfed large web sites knows how easy losing your sense of direction is (see fig. 1.6).

1.6

Hierarchy paradigms provide a central jumping-off point so that the user can have a more customized experience than with linear paradigms.

One effective method of providing users with a constant sense of where they are in a multimedia title or web page that uses a hierarchical structure is to provide users access to a map. An option that brings up a map or table of contents of the entire project or the branch the user is in enables the user to easily navigate further into the site or backtrack through the site.

A hierarchical structure typically uses a bar of icons, an image map, or a text menu as the navigational center. A series of icons that is graphically linked with each area and is positioned in a consistent place on the screen serves as the paradigm by which the user navigates the project. Each level can have a series of areas or pages that are navigated in a linear structure. These levels may require buttons for forward and backward navigation through the site.

Virtual Space

Virtual space is a complex architecture and is mostly common only to games because each direction that a user is allowed to move must be rendered. In the real world, a user can travel in 360 degrees (more if you consider fractions of degrees). Because rendering 360 variations at any given point is not usually possible, the user is typically given up to eight possible directions (North, South, East, West, Northwest, Southwest, Northeast and Southeast). Some virtual projects provide a way for users to look up and down as well. Programs such as Metatool's Bryce and many 3D animation applications do allow for 360 views, but even these environments are usually limited to predefined parameters because of resource limitations. See fig. 1.7.

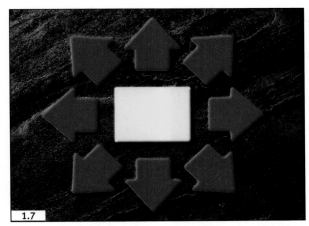

1.7

Virtual space provides for the widest range of possibili-ties, but can also be the most difficult type of paradigm to create.

Whereas virtual spaces are more commonly associated with multimedia titles, web sites are increasingly delivering this paradigm with a combination of creative HTML coding, VRML (Virtual Reality Modeling Language) technology, and Shockwave technology. This structure can easily be both the most confusing and most interesting of the common types of architectures. Because getting lost is easy, these new technologies do not work well as business applications. Virtual space, however, can be effective for educational and entertainment projects.

Because interface designers don't want to give up the space that would be required for 8–10 directional buttons, cursors are among the most common navigational elements used in virtual spaces. The cursor changes into an arrow, hand, or other direction-indicating cursor when the mouse rolls over a pre-defined area on the screen. The user merely clicks the mouse when the cursor displays the direction in which he wants to go. Other creative navigational solutions use a compass-like button that enables users to click on the desired direction in which they want to travel.

Combining Paradigms

Multimedia titles are not limited to any one approach. In fact, most interesting titles utilize a mixture of architectures to take advantage of their various strengths depending on the desired impact of the content. A linear architecture, for instance, can be made to launch into a small virtual space before continuing on; a hierarchical structure can be the launching point for a series of virtual spaces, linear storylines, and other hierarchies.

Multiple paradigms provide the greatest challenges to interface designers who want to maintain a high level of consistency throughout the experience. Global metaphors for multiple architectures are much more challenging to devise and getting the overall perspective of the project can be more difficult to storyboard or flowchart.

Whatever architecture is used, the interface designer must attempt to make the navigation and overall experience as intuitive and enjoyable as possible. A balance between an attractive, user-friendly interface and interesting content is often the recipe for success.

The Sketch

Interfaces are often designed dynamically. It is usually more efficient to design an interface on paper before implementing it on the computer. Sketches are particularly handy for the phase of the design in which the designer is trying to determine the size and placement of elements. Designers can quickly weed out possibilities by sketching the elements and dissecting their weaknesses.

Vector-based applications such as Adobe Illustrator, Macromedia FreeHand, and CorelDRAW! are useful for working out ideas as well (see fig. 1.8). The capability of these applications to quickly draw precise shapes and position them accurately makes them good alternative "sketching" utilities. As shown in some of the projects throughout this book, these vector-based sketches can also be used as templates, starting points, and even channels and layers for interfaces. See Chapter 11, "Vector and 3D Imagery," for more on using vector-based imagery as templates.

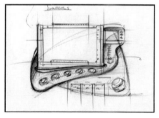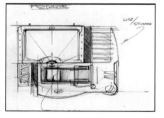
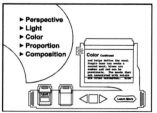

Kyle Anderson, art director at Human Code, used these pencil sketches to work out the various design requirements for his interfaces. The vector-based sketches were used for some of the interfaces in this book.

This chapter presented a general overview of the common elements of interface design. These elements will be expanded and discussed in detail in the following chapters. The next chapter focuses on keeping file sizes small, using various techniques to generate graphics for web interfaces, and using Photoshop's Adjust tools to your best advantage.

CHAPTER 2

RGB Imagery and Palettes

Very little has been written on the subject of RGB imagery, especially as it relates to Photoshop. The beauty and simplicity of working in RGB space can perhaps best be appreciated by designers who have made the transition from the world of print. Graphic designers found that the resource-hungry Photoshop worked much better at 72 ppi in RGB mode than it did at 300 ppi in CMYK mode, making the shift from print to new media enticing. By working with images whose file sizes rarely exceed a couple of megabytes (including layers and channels), designers have much more freedom to explore effects and variations within the constraints of their resources and deadlines. The capability to use layers and channels liberally provides more creative control and the capability to make alterations quickly and easily. Possibly the most appealing aspect of graphic design for multimedia and the web, however, is the immediate feedback. This immediacy enables designers to view their creations in their final media in minutes and days instead of days and weeks.

Covered in this chapter:

- ► Indexing

- ► Bit Depth

- ► Palette Options

- ► Color and Image Size Reduction Strategies

- ► Using Photoshop's Curves to Control Effects

- ► Palette Flashing

- ► Photoshop and the Web

The RGB world does has its own series of challenges. The main problem that multimedia and the web have traditionally faced is the capability of the market in general. Multimedia developers must generate titles that can be viewed on as many computers as possible to make a profit. Unfortunately, the lion's share of the market has only 8-bit color cards, and 8–16 MB of RAM is fairly common. Web developers face similar limitations. Many surfers are riding those 14.4 modems with their 8-bit color card boards. While the processor wars are waging on—resulting in increasing baseline standards in the mass market—developers are still well-advised to produce under the assumption of a modestly equipped market.

Until the general market matures into a more capable standard, developers will likely limit their potential market substantially if they create a multimedia title with full screen 16-bit video or a web page with full page 16-bit graphics. Kiosk and CD-based multimedia development affords a little more latitude because a dedicated system or CD-ROM drive can currently deliver media more efficiently. ISDN, broadband solutions, Shockwave, and other Internet delivery technologies, however, are making cyberspace increasingly attractive and viable to more established multimedia delivery vehicles. In fact, if the Internet continues its amazing growth, it will likely emerge as the vehicle of choice for many multimedia tasks as the market's average capabilities increase.

RGB stands for Red, Green, and Blue. Often, the terms 24-bit and RGB are used interchangeably. With RGB the computer uses the monitor to display 256 shades of red, green, and blue. These three colors are used in various combinations to render up to 16,777,216 colors—if the image requires that many and if the video card can process that many. Current technology can handle these kinds of numbers, but not everyone has been able to keep up with current technology, thereby forcing developers to go to 8-bit color.

Most multimedia and web imagery will be delivered utilizing a limited palette in a low bit depth. Most of the production, however, is often done in 24-bit RGB mode because layers, filters, and other Photoshop functions do not operate in indexed color mode. After the interface designer achieves the desired look, he can reduce the bit depth and then optimize the palette (or optimize the palette and then reduce the bit-depth).

Indexing

The process of reducing 24-bit colors to 8-bit and below is known as *indexing*. The computer attempts to select 256 colors from more than 16 million. The result of this selection is stored in a *color look-up table* (CLUT)—a 16×16 square grid of the 256 colors numbered from 0 to 255. Each color is assigned an RGB color value, and each pixel on the screen is indexed to one of the colors in the CLUT. In Photoshop, you convert a 24-bit image to a 1–8-bit image by selecting Indexed Color from the Mode menu. After converting the image to 1–8-bit color depth, you can view the CLUT by selecting Color Table from the Mode menu.

Optimizing palettes and CLUTs so that images look the same universally is complicated by the fact that systems display images differently. Most operating systems—OS/2, Windows, the Mac OS, and so on—use color managers that come up with creative ways to display images using limited palettes. The problem is that if a display card can only display 256 colors, and an image takes all 256 colors, the elements of the operating system might constantly display with different colors because of the various CLUTs. Most systems do not allow this in most cases, so color managers come up with clever approaches to keep things palettable. To make matters worse, each web browser uses its own palette. Thus, complete control over how images are displayed, especially over the web, is difficult to attain.

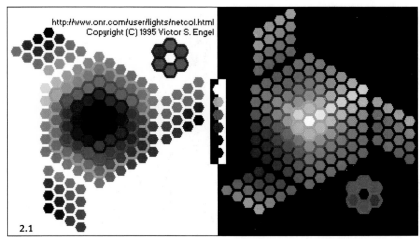

In addition to differences in various platform system palettes, many browsers, including Netscape, use their own color palette to display images from the web.

Bit Depth

Although complete control over how your images appear is somewhere between very difficult and impossible to achieve, elements do exist that you can manipulate to maximize the potential for your images. Typically a 24-bit image dithers to a murky mess when viewed with an 8-bit color card. Designers can control how the image looks by optimizing the palette of the image when reducing its bit depth. The nice thing about 1–8 bit images is that they result in smaller file sizes. File size is an important consideration for both multimedia and web mediums. Web graphics have to travel typically 14.4 to 28.8 bits at a time (actually less, due to bandwidth limitations). Multimedia imagery is loaded into RAM, as is imagery from the web. The difference is that most multimedia titles load many images (and other media) into RAM. Therefore, the more efficient the imagery is, the more efficient the multimedia title runs.

Bit depth refers to the number of colors in an image's palette. Multimedia tends to deal in 2-, 4-, 8-, and 24-bit depths with 8-bit currently being the overwhelming majority. The web can deliver any bit depth you have the patience to download, but 8-bits and lower ensures the widest audience. On the web, no good reason exists for delivering an image in 8-bit when the image contains only 32 colors. Some images need all the colors you can muster, but many can be delivered with relatively few colors. It all boils down to a constant attempt to balance quality with size.

The following chart breaks down bit depths to their colors and image file sizes using an example image that was a 640×480 image at 72 ppi saved in GIF format. GIF files can only be 8-bit and below, but a 24-bit TIFF is 900 KB. These numbers are for illustration purposes only; results may vary.

NUMBER OF BITS	NUMBER OF COLORS	FILE SIZE
24-bit	16.7+ million colors	900 KB
8-bit	256 colors	196 KB
7-bit	128 colors	162 KB
6-bit	64 colors	128 KB
5-bit	32 colors	102 KB
4-bit	16 colors	77 KB
3-bit	8 colors	60 KB
2-bit	4 colors	44 KB
1-bit	2 colors	26 KB

The Bandwidth Conservation Society maintains an excellent site on the Internet (www.infohiway/faster/index.html) with valuable updated information on palettes, bit depth, and strategies for optimizing images for the web.

Palette Options

This section discusses four of Photoshop's palette options:

► System Palettes

► Adaptive Palettes

► Custom Palettes

► Previous Palettes

The choices you make depend upon the overall approach you are taking with the project. If you are using a global palette, you need to choose the System Palette or a Custom Palette. If you are creating images for the web, you can use an Adaptive Palette.

2.2

This image from the Corel Professional Photos collection is colorful and thus demonstrates somewhat exaggerated examples of the result of converting to System and Adaptive palettes.

2.3

8-bit System Palette with Diffusion dithering.

2.4

8-bit Adaptive Palette with Diffusion dithering.

System Palettes

The System Palette option indexes to your platform's default 8-bit color table, which is based on a uniform sampling of RGB colors. The System Palette option is labeled Uniform if the resolution is set to fewer than 8 bits per pixel. Neither option is ideal, but they are often serviceable. The System Palette option is the only option that enables you to use Pattern Dithering in addition to None and Diffusion. Global palettes—palettes that are used for a series of images—do not require the same dithering approach. Experiment to determine which one does the best job.

Windows sets aside the first 10 and the last 10 colors on the System Palette for itself, whereas other operating systems, such as a Macintosh, do not have such a requirement. If a title is developed using a Macintosh palette that does not include some or all of the 20 Windows colors, a portion of the coloring may appear incorrectly on Windows machines. It is common, therefore, for multimedia developers who want to ship cross-platform titles to develop them using the Windows System Palette or at least a Custom Palette with the 20 colors that Windows requires.

After an image is indexed, it cannot be returned to RGB mode with its original 16 million colors. Although regrettable, the image's "non-return" policy can be taken advantage of. For instance, palette control on the web is often considered less urgent than in multimedia, but palette control is certainly not less important. If you want to go to extraordinary measures to have control over how your web images appear and have them appear the same on both the Mac OS and Windows, you can index the image to the Windows System Palette, convert it back to RGB, and then index the image again if you want to go to a lower bit depth. This ensures that all your images—no matter how low their bit depths—are using the same colors.

Adaptive Palettes

Using an Adaptive Palette, Photoshop generates a palette that renders the image as close to the original as possible. Photoshop does this by sampling colors from the more commonly used areas of the color spectrum that appear in the image. For example, if you have an RGB image that contains only the colors red and yellow, the resulting color table is made up primarily of red and yellow colors. Adaptive palettes tend to produce better representations of the original image because colors in most images are concentrated in particular areas of the spectrum.

Controlling how Photoshop builds the Adaptive color table is possible by selecting a part of the image that contains the colors you want to use in the table before you index the image. When you have an active selection in the image, Photoshop weights the conversion toward the colors in the selection. Unless you are going for a posterized look, diffusion is usually the better choice.

You might be tempted to use Adaptive Palettes for web graphics, thinking that global palettes seem to be less of an issue on the web, when in fact most browsers cannot use custom palettes. Therefore, using Adaptive Palettes for images designed for an 8-bit display is a bad idea. Adaptive Palettes look better than the System Palette, however, on 16- and 24-bit display cards.

Custom Palettes

The Custom Palette option enables you to index an image to a custom palette. To generate a custom palette from any image, select Color Table from Mode menu, then select Save. The resulting ACT files can be used cross platform. You can edit palettes in the Color Table dialog box by clicking on a color, and then selecting color values in the Color Picker dialog box. You can click and drag on a series of colors in the Color Table to blend two colors. The Color Picker dialog box displays for the beginning and ending colors in the selection, and the intermediate colors blend the two colors that you choose.

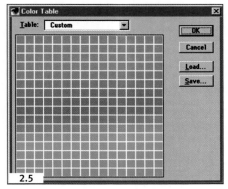

A Custom Palette blended from red to green.

One strategy for creating custom color palettes is to save an Adaptive Palette from an image that contains the most colors you want to include in the custom global palette, and then load this palette as a Custom Palette for the rest of the images. Because editing Custom Palettes can be extremely time consuming, System Palettes are often used.

Previous Palettes

The Previous Palette option is available only after you have indexed an image using the Custom or Adaptive Palette options. Selecting the Previous Palette option converts the image by using the Custom Palette from the previous conversion. This option makes converting a series of images using the same Custom Palette easy.

Color and Image Size Reduction Strategies

Most images do not suffer dramatic quality loss when reduced to 256 colors. Although it takes 256 shades to render a smooth transition from black to white, many images do not have such an extreme contrast. A high-contrast image with dozens of colors all around the color wheel logically suffers from weeding out 16,776,960 colors (16,777,216–256). A large number of images, however, are concentrated in a few color ranges. Preserving the color integrity of the image is not always desired, however. Multimedia and web imagery thrive on special effects and unique renditions of images.

An interface designer can take advantage of these facts by either using images that are in a particular color range for a global palette, grouping images for use with multiple palettes, altering images so that they fit into a desired palette, or designing a visual effects-oriented theme that accommodates a particular palette. The techniques in the following sections are among the strategies that an interface designer can use to reduce the colors and file size of an image.

Too many pixels exist in any given image to spend time being overly precise, but you can provide yourself with a sampling of colors to shoot for. Open an image that utilizes the color palette that you will be using. Select the Info palette from the Window and Palettes menu and drag the cursor over various areas to observe the RGB values. Check out the dominant color themes within the image. You can then use these values as targets for the images you will be altering by adjusting the images so that they contain similar RGB values. This can be done with Hue/Saturation, Color Balance, Levels, Curves, Brightness/Contrast, and by using some of the methods discussed in the following paragraphs. Getting close is usually good enough. After an image is in the ballpark, you can let Photoshop do the rest of the work when it indexes the image.

Color reduction strategies that utilize effects such as dithering and posterization should be used for audiences that won't mind the loss of image quality. Markets such as the high technology industry and entertainment industry see so many images that these audiences are more capable of viewing the images positively. The goal in using the imagery is always to augment rather than distract from the message or content—consider your audience before deciding on one of these strategies.

2.6

This image from KPT Power Photos was altered using the Hue/Saturation Adjust feature, which enabled the color changes to be matched to the paint color of the fire hydrant while maintaining the gray colors revealed by the paint scratches.

Using Photoshop's Adjust Tools

Often an image can be tweaked into a color range using the features in the Image, Adjust menu in Photoshop. Images that are too dark can be lightened with Curves and Brightness/Contrast; images that are too saturated can be desaturated with Hue/Saturation. You can even swap out a range of colors using the Replace Colors feature. Little rocket science is involved with these filters, with the possible exception of the Curves feature. See the following discussion on "Using Photoshop's Curves to Control Effects" and Chapter 12, "Working with Stock Images in Interface Design," for more on using Curves. Again, the object is not to be absolutely precise, but rather to be close enough for Photoshop's conversion to be acceptable or desirable.

A more radical alteration can be made with the Hue/Saturation's colorize feature. Colorizing an image amounts to an on-screen monotone image. When you choose Colorize in the Hue/Saturation dialog box, all colors in the image are reset to 100% saturated red (the 0-degree point on the color wheel). The rotation value you specify by using the hue slider is measured from that point of origin. You can reduce the saturation and vary the lightness value to control the brightness.

Using Duotone Features

Duotones were developed for print, but they can be handy for multimedia and web graphics as well because they pull images into tighter tonal ranges that are more easily indexed. You can create traditional duotone-looking images as well as more extreme effects. To use Photoshop's duotone feature, you must first convert the image to grayscale and then select Duotone from the Mode menu. The Duotone Options dialog box gives you four options: Monotone, Duotone, Tritone, and Quadtone. Monotone effectively duplicates the Hue/Saturation Colorize feature, so the Duotone mode is most effective for Duotone, Tritone, and Quadtone effects.

2.7

A standard duotone look is achieved with this image from CMCD by converting the image to grayscale and then Duotone mode. Index the colors after applying the duotone curves.

You can create a standard duotone by selecting Duotone from the Type menu in the Duotone Options dialog box. Select black and one other color. Reduce the midtones of the black color by dragging the middle of the curve to the lower right, and exaggerate the other color by dragging the middle of the curve to the upper left. Keep in mind that monitors display in only 72–96 ppi; therefore, most effects need to be exaggerated a little. After you achieve the desired duotone effect, select RGB mode and then Indexed Color from the Mode menu.

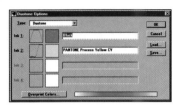

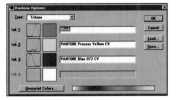

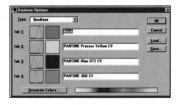

2.8

A more interesting series of effects can be generated by using radical curves.

2.9

This image can now be reduced to as low as 4 bits with hardly noticeable image quality loss.

You can achieve a more interesting series of effects by using radical curves. Avoid muddy areas by giving each color its own tonal range. Exaggerate the curve within a specific range in different areas for each color. Again, after you achieve the desired effect, index the image. Many of these duotone effect images can be reduced to as low as 4 bits with hardly noticeable degradation.

Posterizing

Posterizing reduces the number of colors in an image to a defined number by polarizing groups of colors, resulting in fewer colors to deal with when indexing. Indexing can result in a certain amount of posterizing. You have more control over the posterization, though, with Photoshop's Posterize feature, especially when used in conjunction with Curves as discussed following. To apply posterization, select Posterize from the Image, Map menu. A setting of 3–4 creates a fairly extreme effect that can easily be indexed to as low as 4 bits without noticeable changes from the posterized look. Other effects that reduce the number of colors in an image include Solarize, Trace Contour, Despeckle, Adobe Gallery Effects' Poster Edge, and KPT Edge.

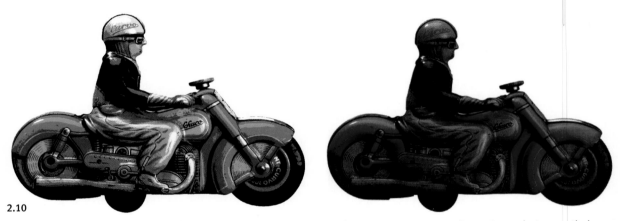

2.10

A posterization level of 3 applied to this image from KPT Power Photos creates a somewhat extreme but nevertheless attractive effect. This image was reduced to 4 bits without noticeable change.

You can create more subtle effects by using a higher posterization setting. In the following example, a setting of 10 was used. With more colors to work with, the polarization is less noticeable. The first image shows the image converted directly to 4 bits with no effects applied. The second image shows what the image looks like when reduced to 4 bits after having a level 10 posterization applied. The difference is not very pronounced, but the posterization method provides a richer image that is slightly less degraded.

2.11

Before applying a posterization level of 10.

2.12

After applying a posterization level of 10.

Using Photoshop's Curves to Control Effects

You can control the effect of the previous strategies by utilizing Photoshop's curves. Converting the image to CMYK provides the most control, but sometimes RGB is more useful depending upon what colors are dominant in the image. The basic idea is to manipulate the curves so that the more important colors are exaggerated. By augmenting particular color ranges in each color channel, you can control where an image is posterized and dithered as well as how the image is indexed.

2.13

The CMYK curves from this image were manipulated so that the red and pale yellow colors stand out more. The green jacket was given more contrast, and much of the black was removed except for where it was needed—in the tires.

2.14

These images have both been indexed to 3 bits. Notice how the original image is drab and lacks contrast. The image with manipulated curves has much more contrast and visual appeal.

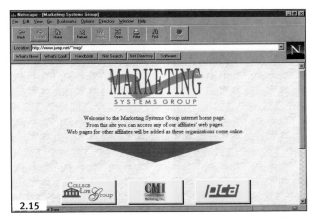

2.15

The tile background for this Marketing System Group's web site was created by reducing the contrast of the seamless tile with Curves before reducing its bit depth.

These techniques are particularly effective for web graphics. Tile backgrounds for web pages, for example, can be altered from stock tile collections so that they are attractive and quick to download. The tile background for this web site is from Visual Software's Textures for Professionals. By manipulating its curves before indexing it, this texture was made subtle and attractive, even though it only has 16 colors and is a mere 5 KB.

Using any one of these strategies can help group colors in your images so that they survive the transition to indexing with more visual integrity. Analyze your site's overall image and theme and then pursue a strategy that fits in with your particular scheme. A duotoned strategy may not fit in with your site's theme if it relies on bright, vivid colors. In any event, it can pay to spend a little extra time preparing your images before you index them.

Palette Flashing

In a project that is designed to display on 8-bit color cards, only one palette may be used at a time. When one palette is replaced with another, the images on the screen are briefly remapped to the new palette, thereby causing an often undesirable "flashing." Two ways exist to prevent this: fade to a color common to both palettes so that no flashing occurs between the transition in a multimedia title, or use one palette globally throughout the project. Utilities such as Equilibrium DeBabelizer can analyze a series of images and suggest a palette that will best portray the images.

If the images in a given project are colorful along a wide spectrum, then a global palette is stretched thin and has a difficult time rendering all the images attractively. One strategy is to use themes. Divide the project into sections, with each having a focused palette. For instance, one theme or section of a project might contain imagery mostly concentrated with dark, rich reds and oranges; another might focus on bright greens and blues.

Photoshop and the Web

The previous discussion largely deals with issues that are common to both multimedia and web imagery. Now, take a look at a few issues specific to using Photoshop to prepare imagery for the web. Photoshop's role in web design and even as an interface design tool for web graphics is largely supportive. Photoshop 3.04 doesn't code pages—it simply processes images. Although using Photoshop to create and process imagery that is 72–100 ppi with 2–256 colors can be seen as using the Rolls Royce to deliver the mail, Photoshop is nevertheless one of the most competent applications for generating web imagery.

It comes down to speed.

One of the most prominent considerations for generating imagery for the web is the final file size of each image. Prevailing market wisdom for the Internet prescribes that web page developers reduce their imagery to the lowest common denominator. Current dogma assumes most web surfers continue to access the web via a 14.4 modem and view their pages with 16-256 colors. Thus, presuming that the widest possible audience is desired, designers are usually encouraged to outfit their web pages with imagery that has substantial constraints on them, so that the lowest end user can receive the information efficiently.

A modem works by emitting and receiving a series of beeps. A 28.8 modem is sending or receiving extremely fast beeps. These beeps are traveling over phone wires that have the same limitations that you experience when you call a friend long distance. Sometimes the connection can be great, sometimes it can be horrible. Because of connection difficulties and many other factors, a 28.8 modem may not actually be able to transfer or receive data at 28.8 kilobytes per second. Here's a list of approximate download times for the three most common channels:

A 14.4 modem transfers data at about 1.5 KB per second on the average.

50 KB	33 seconds
500 KB	5 minutes 31 seconds
1	11 minutes 25 seconds

A 28.8 modem transfers data at about 3 KB per second on the average.

50 KB	17 seconds
500 KB	2 minutes 46 seconds
1 MB	5 minutes 39 seconds

Using an ISDN (56 kbps) line data transfers at about 6 KB per second on the average.

50 KB	8 seconds
500 KB	1 minute 23 seconds
1 MB	2 minutes 51 seconds

These figures are ballpark figures and are designed to help a web designer determine how much time it will take for the average prospective user to view their pages. The strategy is quite simple. Web designers must determine at what speed their desired audience will likely be accessing their pages and design their pages and graphics to be delivered in the quickest amount of time possible for that target audience. For example, web page designers must ask themselves, "Will my audience wait 33 seconds for my 50 KB home page to download?"

If you don't think your audience is going to wait much longer than 30 seconds to view your web page, then a 640×480, 72 dpi, 256 color interface that weighs in at 300 KB is out of the question. Thus, the web page designer must operate with limitations and get creative to balance delivery speed with the aesthetics of a web page.

File Size Factors

► Bit Depth

► Image Size and Resolution

► File Format: JPEG versus GIF

Bit Depth

One major factor that determines the file size of an image is the bit depth. Decreasing bit depth is one of the most important tools a designer has for generating smaller file sizes. Not all web imagery needs to be created with millions of colors. Attractive web interfaces can be generated with as few as 16 colors (4-bit). Use solid colors whenever possible and avoid gradations.

Image Size and Resolution

Avoid making images unnecessarily large. Imagemaps and banners do not need to span the viewer's screen. Icons and banners should obviously be legible, but there's typically no reason to have a two-inch icon that can be viewed reasonably at one inch.

For web imagery, resolution is a factor of the user's monitor and what screen resolution the user is viewing your page with. Most Macintosh monitors display at 72 ppi, PC monitors at 96 ppi, and Unix at up to 100 ppi. If your image is 72 ppi, it appears smaller on a Unix monitor than a Macintosh monitor. Likewise, if a web surfer's video card is set at 800×600, the web page appears smaller than if viewed at 640×480.

File Format: JPEG versus GIF

File compression formats are one of the keys to generating small images for the web. The two leading formats commonly used are JPEG and GIF. As a quick rule of thumb, JPEGs should be used on photographic images—images with lots of colors and images with lots of noise—and GIFs should be used for images that have more consistent groupings of colors, such as line art. Of course, there are exceptions to these rules.

JPEG works on 24-bit images to generate compression up to 100:1. The JPEG format, developed by the Joint Photographic Experts Group, works by compressing an image when it is saved and then decompressing it when it is viewed. The decompression time can take a while, so JPEG doesn't always provide a profound advantage over GIF. In addition, as with any lossy compression format (*lossy* is a term used for formats that discard data to achieve compression), JPEG tends to degrade an image more than GIF does. Finally, JPEG does not support transparency. For these reasons, the GIF format enjoys a more prominent role on the web than the JPEG format.

GIF works on 1-8 bit images, converting 24-bit images to at least 8-bit. GIF works by indexing colors along a horizontal axis and referencing them according to groups. If an image has 16 blue pixels in a row, a standard format might refer to them as something such as pixel one blue, pixel two blue, pixel three blue, and so on. GIF stores this information by referring to them as something such as pixels 1–16 blue. This approach has its obvious limitations. For example, if every other color is a different color, then it's harder for GIF to compress the image. However, because GIF 89a supports transparency and interleaving and uses dithering instead of outright throwing out data like JPEG does, GIF is more commonly used.

Obviously the ideal is to use each format for its strengths and weaknesses. It's worth taking the time to try JPEGs and GIFs at various qualities and bit-depths respectively to see which generates the best balance between image results and file size reduction.

Imagemaps

Three main ways exist of delivering graphic interfaces on the web. You can generate a series of small icons accompanied by HTML text and tags, you can generate an imagemap, and you can use a plug-in/multimedia solution such as Shockwave. Using small icons provides the least amount of control because each browser lays them out differently. Technologies, such as Shockwave, are certainly becoming more appealing, but they require that the user have the plug-in, and "Shocked" and similar files can get big quickly.

An *imagemap* is an image that has a map associated with it that tells the browser to do things or go places depending upon where the user clicks on it. Imagemaps can be any size, orientation, resolution, and bit depth. An imagemap requires a graphic, a map file, a tag in the HTML code that tells the browser that the graphic is an imagemapped graphic, and either a short program (such as a CGI script) that runs on the server or a feature within the browser that coordinates the graphic with the map to function according to the user's clicks.

The graphic image itself is largely useless without the map. A map file matches pixel coordinates to URL links or other functions such as e-mail. When a user clicks within the coordinates, the browser responds according to the function mapped to those coordinates. Map files are simply ASCII (text only) files. A mapped file is often referred to as a *hotspot*. The entire imagemap is a series of hotspots.

An imagemap created with minimal colors for quick download (not actual size according to example).

Following is an example of what a map file might look like for an imagemap.

default home.htm		
rect design.htm	0,0	200,200
rect music.htm	0,250	200,450
rect bibio.htm	250,0	450,200
rect info.htm	250,250	450,450

The first line in a map file defines the default URL. If a user clicks on the imagemap, but does not click within the specific mapped areas, the browser responds according to the default. Each subsequent line maps coordinates according to three designations: the shape, the URL, and the pixel coordinates. A hotspot can be a rectangle, circle, or polygon, denoted "rect," "circle," or "poly" respectively.

Pixel coordinates are listed as "x,y" (across and down) coordinate pairs separated by a comma. The coordinates describe the parameters for the shape. Each shape uses different parameters. A rectangle is defined by the upper left and lower right parameters. A circle is defined by its lower right X and upper left Y coordinates, with a third coordinate to define its radius. A polygon is defined by each point of direction change on the boundaries of the polygon.

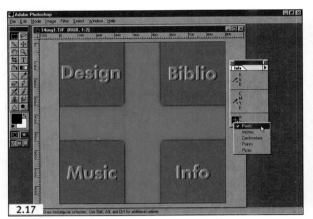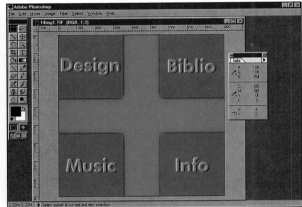

Use the Info Palette to determine pixel coordinates. Be sure to change the units to pixels.

Photoshop 3.05 does not build imagemap map files. Although shareware utilities such as Mapedit for Windows and WebMap for the Mac are readily available, however, it is entirely possible to create map files with Photoshop and any text editor that exports an ASCII file. In Photoshop, open the Info Palette (Window, Palette). If the X,Y values are not in pixels, click on the right pointing arrow within the crosshairs icon and change the value to pixels. Now drag your cursor over the image to get the pixel coordinates.

Using the LOWSRC Extension

One final tidbit for imagemaps. Netscape's LOWSRC extension provides some helpful and interesting possibilities. This tag was created so that web designers could use a smaller file size version of an image to display first and then replace the smaller file size version with a larger one after it loads. If a browser doesn't support the extension, it merely displays the main image. Here's an example of how a LOWSRC extension might look:

<IMG SRC="interface.gif" LOWSRC="quickie.gif">

LOWSRC is handy for large imagemaps. A black-and-white version, for example, can be generated to load first so that the viewer can more quickly view the options. You don't have to use the same image for the main image and the LOWSRC—you can also have a small "please wait" graphic display.

Using the GIF89a Export Plug-In

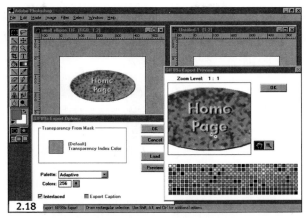

The GIF89a export plug-in supports transparency colors from RGB images.

Adobe 3.05 ships with the GIF89a plug-in, which supports transparency and interlacing for GIF files. Adobe 3.04 (the export filter doesn't work for earlier versions) users can download the GIF89a export plug-in filter at http://www.adobe.com/Software.html.

If you have the GIF89a filter loaded, select GIF89a Export from the File, Export menu. Users cannot choose the transparency color when exporting from RGB mode. The dialog box allows for reduction of colors, interlacing, and preview, but not for choosing or changing the transparency color. It is defaulted at 128 RGB. The Preview enables you to zoom and pan, but not customize the transparency.

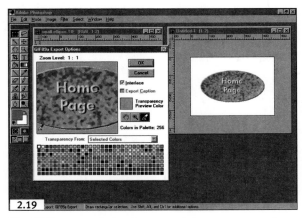

The GIF89a export plug-in supports transparency colors from indexed images.

Using the GIF89a with an indexed images does not enable further bit–depth reduction, but a complete set of transparency controls does exist. Use the Eyedropper tool to select colors for transparency either from the image or from the color swatches. Select multiple colors from the image or color swatches to add to the number of colors that will be transparent. Hold down the Ctrl or Command key to deselect colors. Click on the Transparency Color Preview swatch to change the preview color. Hold down the spacebar to temporarily access the Pan tool.

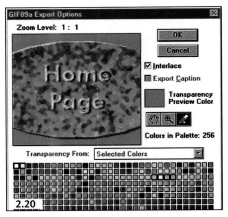

You can add and subtract additional transparency colors as well as change the preview color for the cumulative transparency effect.

The capability to use multiple colors for transparency makes it easier to avoid haloing. Colors selected for transparency have a bold outline around them in the swatch index. Use a distinct preview color to help determine whether or not you are inadvertently making areas of the image transparent that you don't want to.

Seamless Tiles

Beyond using a different background color than gray with a hexadecimal designation, seamless tiles are one of the best ways to add flavor to a web page without adding excessively to the download time of the entire page. The key is to use a small tile with a low bit depth.

Tiles need not be square. A rectangular tile with alternating solid colors, for instance, can be just as effective as a square tile. Rectangular tiles need be only a few pixels high. Random patterns such as noises tile fairly well, and a seamless tile collection such as Pixar 128 can be easily converted to lower bit depths.

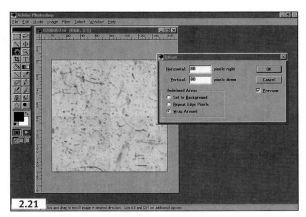

Use the Offset filter to generate seamless tiles.

Use Offset (Filter, Other) on an RGB texture to generate seamless patterns from non-seamless textures. This texture was cropped to 160 pixels square from a Kai's Power Photo texture (typically a smaller tile would be more appropriate). By offsetting half the image size vertically and horizontally with the Wrap Around option selected, Offset does most of the work necessary to create a seamless tile. Touch up the seams within the tile with the Rubber Stamp and Smudge tools.

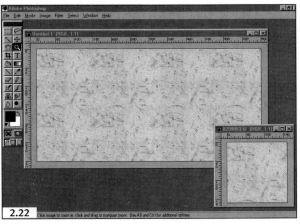

Preview the seamless texture by filling a large file with the tile as a pattern.

To preview how the tile will look, Select All, and select Define Pattern from the Edit menu. Create a larger file for the pattern to tile into and fill the file with the pattern (Edit, Fill, Pattern). When you are happy with the file, index it and reduce the bit depth to as low as possible.

Specing Hex Colors

With a scientific calculator, you can spec hexadecimal colors with Photoshop.

Web browsers specify colors using hexadecimal code. To coordinate these colors with images that you generate with Photoshop, you can use RGB values that you get from Photoshop's Info Palette or Color Picker dialog box with a scientific calculator (Windows users have a Scientific mode on their calculator) to determine the hexadecimal codes. Enter the numeral in Decimal mode and then change the mode to Hexadecimal mode to get the hexadecimal equivalent. Each RGB value must be entered individually. Hexadecimal numbers are listed in RGB order. Red 255 (FF in hexadecimal), Green 153 (99 in hexadecimal), and Blue 51 (33 in hexadecimal) would be listed as FF9933 in hexadecimal.

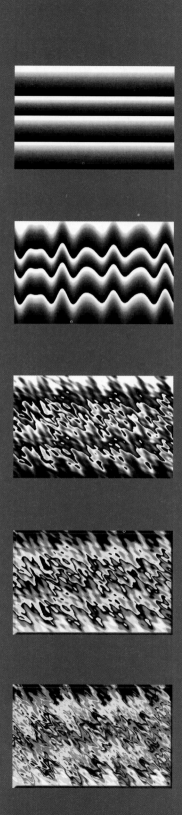

CHAPTER 3

Textures from Scratch

Effective use of texture can be an efficient way to add visual interest to various multimedia and web elements. Often what makes nature so intriguing is its endless texture. Many people find texture to be more visually appealing than solid colors, although solid colors can provide nice contrast to a texture-filled environment.

Although there is a wealth of third-party textures available on CD-ROM, on the Internet, and within nature itself, Photoshop can often be used to generate many of the textures needed in interface design. Photoshop's proprietary filters and features provide a wide variety of possibilities, but with a few common third-party filters, you can generate an endless variety of textures from scratch.

Covered in this chapter:

► Creating original textures

► Texture strategies

Creating Original Textures

This chapter attempts to map out possible avenues that are merely jumping off points for more variations. As with any limitless phenomena, generating textures from scratch can be excessively time-consuming. By mapping out many of the possible directions, this chapter shows that generating textures from scratch in Photoshop is a relatively easy process.

Noises and Mezzotints

3.1

Add Noise, Value: 50, Uniform, Mono.

Add Noise, Value: 100, Gaussian, Mono.

Mezzotint, Grainy dots.

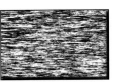
Mezzotint, Medium strokes.

Begin creating your texture by dropping some color into the file. You can change the color later with Hue/Saturation and Color Balance, so precision is not always necessary. Most of the filters need something to work with to generate texture. Photoshop's Add Noise (Filters, Noise) and Mezzotint (Filters, Pixelate) filters provide excellent bases for random textures. With values from 1–999 and two distribution methods, Add Noise offers more variety. With Mezzotint, you simply have 10 choices to choose from, each of which can generate unique strains of textures. The Uniform distribution method produces a more subtle effect by distributing noise by calculating random numbers between 0 and plus or minus the specified value. The Gaussian distribution method utilizes a bell-shaped curve to produce a more pronounced noise effect. The Monochromatic Noise option keeps the tones in the same range as the base color. In general, you can use Monochromatic Uniform or Gaussian noises with smaller values for subtle textures; you can use Monochromatic or non-Monochromatic Gaussian noises and Mezzotints for more pronounced textures. Clouds and Difference Clouds (Filter, Render), KPT Noise f/x, Adobe Gallery Effects' Grain, Texturizer, and Reticulation are also valuable random jumping off points.

Larger Grains

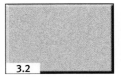
3.2

Sand.

Crystallize 5.

Mosaic 4.

Pointillize 3.

Minimum 1, Hue/ Saturation-Lightness 25.

You can add Monochromatic Noise to a tan color to create a sandy look. Sometimes, Add Noise and related effects create grains that are too small for some effects. Use the Crystallize, Mosaic, and Minimum (with low settings) filters to spread out or enlarge the noise. Many of these textures are subtle and attractive enough to be used with interfaces and buttons.

Brushed Metals

Motion Blur–45, distance 20 on Add Noise Uniform 50, Mono.

Same on Add Noise Gaussian 100 Mono.

Brushed Metal.

Brushed Brass.

Brushed Copper.

You can create a subtle, yet attractive texture by simply adding a Motion Blur. Motion Blurs added to subtle noises tend to generate a brushed look, whereas Motion Blurs added to more pronounced noises create a somewhat painted look. This effect is commonly used for generating various brushed metal looks by using various metallic colors as the base color.

Stuccos

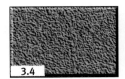

Gaussian Blur 1.5, AGE Emboss 15.

From Add Noise Gaussian 200.

Photoshop's emboss overlaid on solid blue.

Mezzotint, Grainy Dots, with highest emboss setting.

Two stucco effects combined with Darken mode.

To generate various stucco effects, add a little Gaussian Blur to a noise, and then emboss it. Both Adobe Gallery Effects and KPT Convolver will maintain the color when embossing; Photoshop's Emboss filter will turn everything gray. You can emboss with Photoshop's Emboss filter, and then use the results with Overlay mode over a solid color to get results similar to those produced from third-party filters. More pronounced noises produce more contrast. Attractive variations can be generated from Mezzotints by using extreme emboss settings and by combining multiple stucco effects with layer modes.

More Stucco

Find Edges with Multiply mode.

Ripple with Darken mode.

Trace Contour with Difference Mode 15% opacity.

AGE Sponge with Darken 50% opacity.

AGE Fresco with Darken 50% opacity.

You can create unique "stucco" effects by adding a Gaussian Blur and then creating a duplicate layer. By altering the duplicate with various textures and merging it with the original with various modes and opacities, you can generate many stucco variations.

Stuccos with Bump Maps

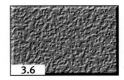

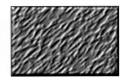

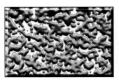

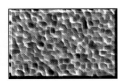

Brightness/Contrast-Contrast 100, Gaussian Blur 1, Emboss 2, Luminosity mode.

AGE Sumi-e, Gaussian Blur 2, Emboss 3, Luminosity.

Brightness/Contrast-Contrast 100, Gaussian Blur 2, Adobe Gallery Effects' Plaster, Luminosity.

Brightness/Contrast-Contrast 50, Gaussian Blur 3, Crystallize, Emboss 2, Luminosity.

From a scan, Gaussian Blur 2.5, Emboss, Luminosity.

Some "stucco" or related embossed effects work better when you generate them with "bump maps." The following steps show how to generate a bump map.

1. Create a new layer over the solid color background, fill with white, and then Add Noise and Gaussian before applying various filters. Generating the effects in the higher contrast that black, white, and grayscale tones provide can create useful variations.

2. After creating the "bump map" layer, position it on top of the solid color background layer, and use various modes and opacities to complete the effect.

Bump maps can also be generated from scans and line art.

Antique Stucco

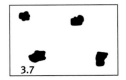

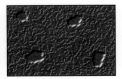

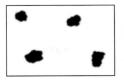

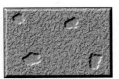

Paint a few random blobs.

Displace, Gaussian Blur.

Emboss.

Mask, delete, and merge.

Hard Light mode over a subtle noise texture.

With a few extra steps, you can antique a stucco pattern.

1. Open a new file, press F7 to open the Layers Palette (if it's not already open, create a new layer (Layer 1)), and draw a few random-shaped black blobs on a white background.

2. Roughen up the blobs a little with Displace (Filter, Distort)—use 2 for the horizontal and vertical displacement, and use the Fragment displacement map located in the plugins\dispmaps directory.

3. Add a Gaussian Blur with a 1–2 radius.

4. Emboss with highlights and shadows opposite the main stucco pattern.

5. Create a duplicate layer (Layer 1 copy), Select all, fill with white, and then generate a grayscale stucco pattern by using one of the previous techniques.

6. Mask out the surrounding 50 percent grays on Layer 1, except those within the blobs, and delete. Be sure the blobs layer is on top (Layer 1 over Layer 1 copy), and then merge the layers.

7. Fill the background layer with a light color, and then Add Noise.

8. Select the Hard Light Mode for Layer 1, and then merge the layers.

Liquefying

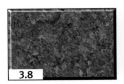

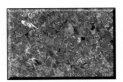

Add Noise, Gaussian Blur, Ripple.

Add Noise, Crystallize, AGE Fresco, Ripple.

Add Noise, Extrude, Ripple.

AGE Stained Glass, Gaussian Blur, Ripple.

Twirl, AGE Chrome, Hue/Saturation Colorize, Ripple.

You can "liquefy" just about anything by using either the Ripple feature or by using a combination of Distortion filters. Typically, the main things to watch out for are too much tonal variation and too much distortion. Liquefying a texture is also an excellent intermediate technique, and extreme distortions can have the effect of wiping out any recognizable aspect of the texture.

Liquid Textures Method 1

Blue gradient.

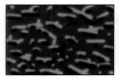

Light blue strokes.

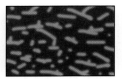

Dark blue strokes.

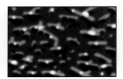

Black-and-white flecks.

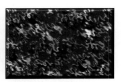

Ripple, Medium, 999.

Generating liquid textures is a good way to learn about the distort filters. You can create a simple wavy liquid texture by laying down a linear gradient at a slight angle.

1. Choose two blues (or whatever color you're liquefying) that are somewhat dark but fairly similar in color. Change the foreground color to a very light color, and paint a series of random strokes with a semi-thick, soft brush.

2. Select a color a few shades darker than the darkest color used in the gradient, and add slightly smaller companion strokes to the light strokes.

3. Add a few random flecks of black and white for contrast.

4. Now Ripple (Filter, Distort) the file with a setting in the 700–999 range on the Medium setting or in the 300–500 range on the Large setting.

Liquid Textures Method 2

Blue gradient.

Light blue strokes.

Dark blue strokes.

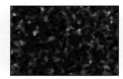

Black-and-white flecks.

Ripple, Medium, 999.

You also can generate liquid textures by using this alternative technique.

1. Start with a dark color and add a monochromatic Gaussian Noise within the 100–150 range.

2. Crystallize (Filter, Pixelate) with a cell size of about 5–10.

3. Use Median (Filter, Noise) with a radius of 5 or 6 to spread out and overlap the colors.

4. Now Ripple (Filter, Distort) the file with a setting in the 700–999 range on the Medium setting or in the 350–550 range on the Large setting.

Liquid Textures Method 3

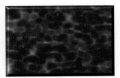

Solid Black. *Mezzotint Medium strokes two times, Maximum 1.* *Gaussian Blur 4.* *Minimum 3.* *Screen mode over dark blue.*

You can generate a much softer liquid texture by using an entirely different approach.

1. Begin with a solid black fill.

2. Apply the Medium strokes Mezzotint (Filter, Pixelate) filter two times, and then apply the Maximum (Filter, Other) filter with a 1-pixel radius.

3. Apply a Gaussian Blur with a radius of 2–5.

4. Apply the Minimum filter (Filter, Other) with a setting of 2–4.

5. Make a duplicate layer, select all, delete the background layer, and then fill it with a medium-dark blue color.

6. Drag the duplicate layer (Layer 1 copy) below Layer 1, and apply the Screen mode to layer 1.

Flame Textures Method 1

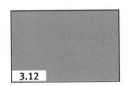

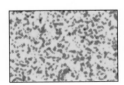

Bright Orange. *Mezzotint Grainy dots.* *Median 2.* *Gaussian Blur 2.* *Ripple, Medium 450.*

One method of creating a flame is very similar to liquefying.

1. Begin with a bright orange color.

2. Add a Grainy dots Mezzotint.

3. Use the Median filter with a radius setting of 2.

4. Add a Gaussian Blur with a radius of about 2.

5. Now add a Medium Ripple with a setting of 250–750 or a Large Ripple with a setting of 150–400.

Flame Textures Method 2

3.13

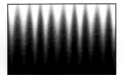

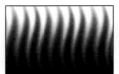

Vertical linear black-to-white gradient.

Wave.

Shear.

Indexed Color, Color Table Black Body, RGB mode.

Curves.

Another method of creating a flame utilizes a different set of filters and generates an entirely different effect.

1. Begin with a black-to-white vertical linear gradient.

2. Apply the Wave (Filter, Distort) filter with anywhere from 3–100 generations, Wavelength 10–20, Amplitude 5–75, and Scale Vertical 25–75 percent (horizontal scale has no effect) with the Repeat Edge Pixels option turned on. Use Shear (Filter, Distort) to distort the flames slightly.

3. Select Indexed Color from the Mode menu, and choose the Custom palette option. In the Color Table dialog box, select Black Body from the pop-up menu. Then convert the file back to RGB.

4. You can use the Curves feature (Image, Adjust) to lower the peaks of the flame by dragging the center down to the lower right.

Flame Textures Method 3

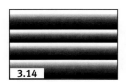
3.14

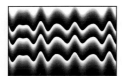

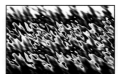

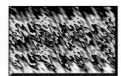

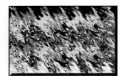

Multiple vertical linear black-to-white gradient.

Wave.

Ripple.

Indexed Color, Color Table Black Body, RGB mode.

Ripple.

An interesting variation of this flame technique can generate multiple gradients.

1. To begin, create a series of rectangle selections by filling each one with a black-to-white vertical linear gradient.

2. Apply the Wave (Filter, Distort) filter with anywhere from 1–5 generations, Wavelength about 10 minimum and 30 maximum, Amplitude about 5 minimum and 25 maximum, and Scale Vertical 25–75 percent (horizontal scale has no effect) with the Repeat Edge Pixels option turned on.

3. Apply the Ripple filter with Medium 900–999 or Large 450–800.

4. Select Indexed Color from the Mode menu, and then select Custom Palette.

5. In the Color Table dialog box, select Black Body from the Table pop-up menu.

6. Convert the file back to RGB.

7. Apply the Median filter with a 4–6 setting, and reapply the Ripple filter to further mix up the flames.

Wood

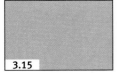    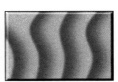

Tan or light brown.	*Mezzotint Grainy dots.*	*Median 2.*	*Gaussian Blur 2.*	*Ripple, Medium 450.*

Here is a simple technique for creating faux wood.

1. Begin with a tan-colored background.

2. Create a duplicate layer, select all, and then delete.

3. Select a darker brown color, and use the Paintbrush tool with a 100-pixel, soft brush.

4. Draw a vertical line by clicking at the top of the file, pressing the Shift key, and clicking at the bottom of the page.

5. Select half of the line, delete, deselect, and then apply a Gaussian Blur at a radius of approximately 3.5.

6. Create several duplicate layers, and spread them out evenly.

7. Use the Shear (Filter, Distort) filter to warp the lines and merge the layers, and use a slight Monochromatic, Uniform Add Noise to add a little grain.

Corrugated Textures

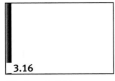    

Horizontal Linear Gradient.	*Horizontal Linear Gradient, Define Pattern.*	*Fill Pattern.*	*Corrugated Metal.*	*Corrugated Cardboard.*

You can generate corrugated textures with the Pattern Fill feature.

1. Begin with a blank, white file.

2. Create a new layer, and then make a vertical selection one-eighth of an inch wide that is as tall as the file (using the rulers helps).

3. Fill the file with a horizontal linear gradient that changes from black on the right side of the file to white on the left.

4. Now create another vertical selection directly adjacent to the first one-eighth of an inch wide. This vertical line needs to be as tall as the file.

5. Fill the file with a horizontal linear gradient that changes from black on the left of the files to white on the right.

6. Select the combined gradients. (If you have done this correctly, your selection should have a width of exactly one-quarter of an inch.)

7. Next select Define Pattern from the Edit menu.

8. Select Fill from the Edit menu, and fill the entire file with the pattern.

9. Generate any texture (such as the Noise textures shown above) on the background layer, and apply the Multiply mode to the corrugated layer.

Pattern Textures

Blinds.

Punched metal surface.

Wallpaper.

Cheap brick wall.

Notched metal surface.

The Pattern fill feature is the feature of choice for any repetitive textures. Patterns can be square, rectangular, tall, and wide. Create patterns from simple black shapes as the basis for emboss effects. When the patterns are generated on white backgrounds, it's easy to select alternated rows and create offsetting patterns. Noised backgrounds can also be offset easily. The preceding example used a pattern created with the Extrude filter.

Stone Wall

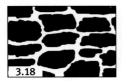

Random blob/rock shapes.

Rock highlights and shadows.

Mortar highlights and shadows.

Mortar.

Stone wall.

INTERFACE DESIGN with Photoshop

Stone textures are a little less automated than most textures.

1. Begin with a blank, white file.

2. Create a new layer named Rocks H&S (for highlights and shadows), and draw a series of random blobs roughly equal distance from one another.

3. Select all, copy, create a new channel, and paste into the channel.

4. Duplicate the layer, and name the duplicate Mortar H&S.

5. Apply a 4–5 radius Gaussian Blur (2–3 for the Mortar H&S layer), and apply the Emboss filter with 4–6 Height (2–3 for the Mortar H&S layer) and approximately 100 Amount.

6. Use approximately 135 degrees for the Rock H&S layer and –45 degrees for the Mortar H&S layer.

7. Use the Eyedropper tool to select a 50 percent gray from somewhere in the embossed Rock H&S layer.

8. Load the selection and press Alt/Option+Delete. Repeat this process for the Mortar H&S layer.

9. Fill the background layer with gray, add Monochromatic Noise, and merge the Mortar H&S layer and the background with the Hard Light mode.

10. Create two duplicate layers of the background and name them Rock Texture and Rock Texture H&S (the Rock Texture H&S layer should be above Rock Texture).

11. On the Rock Texture H&S layer, select all, fill with white, Add Noise, Gaussian Blur, Brightness/Contrast 20 and 40 (respectively), and emboss.

12. Fill the Rock Texture layer with a medium tone color, and merge the Rock Texture and the Rock Texture H&S layers with the Luminosity mode.

13. Adjust the Hue/Saturation to the desired color.

14. Merge the Rock H&S layer with the Rock Texture layer with the Hard Light Mode.

15. Load the selection, delete, deselect, and merge the layers.

Combining Textures

3.19

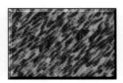

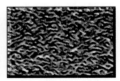

Background: Find Edges, Layer 1: Brightness/Contrast 50, AGE Rough Pastels.

Background: Crystallize, Layer 1: Color Halftone, Motion Blur, Ripple, Difference Cloud, Difference mode.

Background: No change, Layer 1: AGE Sumi-e, Overlay 80%.

Background: Crystallize 50, Ripple Large 700, Invert, Layer 1: Clouds, Ripple Large 450, Difference mode.

Background: Crystallize 10, AGE Fresco, Layer 1: Ripple Large 200, AGE Glass.

You can combine various effects to create other attractive effects. By creating two layers, applying a series of filters to each, and then recombining them, you can generate attractive textures. Although this approach can be slightly more time consuming, it is often helpful to keep the two layers in similar tonal ranges while generating contrasting textures on each layer. All of these examples start with blurred noise.

Textures from Third-Party Filter Sources

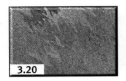  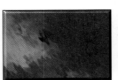  

Background: KPT Texture Explorer, Layer 1: Crystallize 35, Add Noise, Ripple, Luminosity mode.

Background: KPT Texture Explorer, Layer 1: Ripple, Add Noise, AGE Glass, Emboss.

Background: KPT Texture Explorer, Layer 1: Ripple, Wave, Twirl.

Background: KPT Texture Explorer, Layer 1: Add Noise, Crystallize, AGE Emboss.

Background: KPT Texture Explorer, Layer 1: Mezzotint Fine Dots, Colored Pencils.

KPT Texture Explorer textures are easy to spot. What KPT Texture Explorer does provide better than just about any other source is a wealth of random bump maps and gradients that can provide the basis for attractive textures using the previous techniques. Avoid textures with wild psychedelic gradients, or use the Hue/Saturation with the Colorize option filter to reign in the hues. These examples were purposefully kept conservative to demonstrate that results in KPT Texture Explorer do not have to be wild.

Textures from Stock Photo Sources

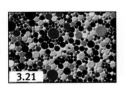  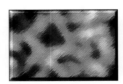  

Image from Photo Disc, Industrial Sidestreets.

Ripple, Hue/Saturation Colorize.

Background: KPT Texture Explorer, Layer 1: Add Noise, Crystallize, AGE Emboss.

Displace, Difference Clouds, Curves.

Mosaic, Wind, Displace 3 times, Curves.

No reason exists why you should have to start completely from scratch. Generating completely different textures from scanned sources or stock imagery is often as easy as generating textures from scratch. In general, source imagery that provides plenty of contrast, the color tones you are looking for, or any particular patterns you might need are good candidates for tweaking with filters. By doing this, you can create useful textures from source imagery.

INTERFACE DESIGN with Photoshop

Texture Strategies

The only way to become efficient with creating textures from scratch is to become familiar with the results of the various filters and the combined filter effects. As time permits, perhaps while you are on the phone or taking a break, experiment with each filter and combinations of filters. Take each filter to its extreme settings, and then observe the results of intermediate settings. Try each filter with various types of images: images with contrast, images with little contrast, blank files, files with noise, colorful images, bland images, and grayscale images. To become familiar with combined effects, try various filters on Noises, Ripples, Mezzotints, and the rest of the filters that generate recognizable effects. Observe the results of multiple applications of each filter. Do not assume that what looks like mud cannot be turned into an attractive texture with a few adjustments.

The less a texture looks like a recognizable effect, the less it will draw unwanted attention to itself. Often, the idea is to create a texture that augments the subject matter without distracting from it. If that is your ideal, try to keep color schemes in one or two attractive tonal ranges. Avoid extreme distortions. Effective textures are typically a balance between randomness and subtle patterns.

You can speed up the experimentation by working with small files. Create a 1–2 inch square file to experiment with. Because many filters are resolution-dependent in terms of the intensity of their effect, experiment in the resolution that you intend to use in your final product. However, experimentation at 72 dpi will certainly provide insight into the results at higher resolutions. While experimenting, create a temporary directory and save attractive results that you can revert back to—taking notes is never a bad idea.

General Notes on Photoshop's Filters for Creating Textures from Scratch

The following sections contain brief notes on Photoshop's filters, what each filter does, and what each filter might work best for. Of course, these findings are based on the author's knowledge and experience. Experiment on your own to discover which filters work best for your projects.

Blur

- Gaussian
- Blur More
- Motion
- Radial
- Blur

Gaussian Blur and Motion Blur are critical filters for texture generation. Use Gaussian Blurs to spread out black pixels for embossing, for muddying colors, and for softening any hard edges. At low resolution, a little Gaussian Blur goes a long way. Motion Blurs can also get out of hand quickly. Extreme distances with Motion Blur can sometimes yield interesting results. Use Blur and Blur More for anti-aliasing. Use Radial Blur for glows and circular highlights.

Distort

- ► Displace
- ► Polar Coordinates
- ► Shear
- ► Twirl
- ► ZigZag
- ► Pinch
- ► Ripple
- ► Spherize
- ► Wave

Displace, Ripple, and Wave are the more general purpose distortion filters used to create textures. Only the Displace filter can generate truly distinctive distortions, especially with custom displacement maps. Look to Displace for random distortions (the fragment, mezzo, and random displacement maps are particularly useful). Mastering the Displace filter adds a valuable tool to a Photoshop user's arsenal. Use Ripple and Wave for "liquefying" textures. Ripple is also useful for quickly making textures unrecognizable and can be used with filters such as Mezzotint and Crystallize to avoid the telltale look of its effect. Shear is handy for horizontal distortions. You can always rotate an object to distort with Shear. The rest of the distortion filters are less subtle, although they can be used to create interesting effects from time to time.

Noise

- ► Add Noise
- ► Dust and Scratches
- ► Despeckle
- ► Median

Add Noise is the foundation for a large majority of textures created from scratch. Use Uniform noises for soft effects and Gaussian noises for more visible effects. Because Add Noise is a random generator, any attempt at precision with this filter is a waste of time. Use Despeckle and Dust and Scratches to de-muddy a texture slightly, or use these filters to dull the effect of noise if you later determine that the texture contains too much noise. Use Median to blend colors, especially in conjunction with most of the Pixellate filters.

Pixellate

- ► Color Halftone
- ► Facet
- ► Mezzotint
- ► Pointillize
- ► Crystallize
- ► Fragment
- ► Mosaic

Crystallize, Mosaic, and Pointillize are good filters for creating larger building blocks for textures: Crystallize for polygons, Mosaic for squares, and Pointillize (and Color Halftone) for circles. Facet is

INTERFACE DESIGN with Photoshop

sort of a subtle Mosaic, but it contains overlapping shapes. Fragment can generate a somewhat slightly distorted textile look. Use the Median, Maximum, Minimum, and Unsharp Mask filters to augment the effects of these filters. The Mezzotint effects are great alternatives to Add Noise. Also look to Mezzotints with solid colors—especially black—for layer effects.

Render

- ► Clouds
- ► Difference Clouds
- ► Lens Flare
- ► Lighting Effects
- ► Texture Fill

Clouds and Difference Clouds are handy for mixing up the brightness levels of textures, especially when applied on a separate layer and merged with various modes. Lighting effects can create some great effects, and can be used for quick lighting controls. Much of what the Lighting Effects filter can do, however, can be done by using the more versatile layers. You can distort Lens Flares for interesting results. Opt for Photoshop's Pattern Fill feature rather than the Texture Fill filter.

Sharpen

- ► Sharpen
- ► Sharpen Edges
- ► Sharpen More
- ► Unsharp Mask

Unsharp Mask is the handiest filter in this bunch. Use these filters to offset over blurring, to polarize gradients in textures, and create edges that are not as pronounced as those generated with the Find Edges and Trace Contour filters. Use Unsharp Mask to augment the results of the Pixellate filters.

Stylize

- ► Diffuse
- ► Emboss
- ► Extrude
- ► Find Edges
- ► Solarize
- ► Tiles
- ► Trace Contour
- ► Wind

Turn to Diffuse and Wind when you need things roughed up without the added noise. Try multiple applications of Diffuse for a more pronounced effect. Photoshop's Emboss is not as robust as most third-party emboss filters, but when used with layers, modes, and channels, this filter can be used to a similar effect with a little more work. Emboss generates interesting and useful effects at high values. Find Edges and Trace Contour generate valuable namesake effects. When one of these two filters doesn't generate quite what you need, try the other. Downplay the results of Solarize with Curves and Hue/Saturation for earth tones. Extrude and Tiles generate one-dimensional effects, but can be useful from time to time.

Video

► Deinterlace ► NTSC Colors

Deinterlace is not just for video, although its value for texture generation is minimal. Unfortunately, its effects are not cumulative. Look to it as an addition to the Pixellate filters for altering noise.

Submenu Options

► Custom ► Highpass

► Maximum ► Minimum

► Offset

Maximum and Minimum are valuable filters. Their names may seem counterintuitive when it comes to black and white. Maximum chokes black; Minimum spreads black. Look at this idea from the perspective of white, and it makes sense. Maximum expands white; Minimum decreases it. High Pass is also valuable for black-and-white and grayscale imagery. High Pass is particularly effective with mask and layer effect generation and can be viewed as the opposite of Gaussian Blur because High Pass emphasizes highlights instead of blurring them. Offset can be useful and fun with color channels. Because of the nearly unlimited potential possibilities, use Custom only when you have a lot of time on your hands.

Image, Map

► Invert ► Equalize

► Threshold ► Posterize

Threshold is extremely valuable for cleaning up noises and creating high contrast for black-and-white images. Equalize generates contrasts while maintaining colors and is very good for brightening muddy textures. Invert is one-dimensional but very useful, and Posterize can turn a bad texture around by reigning in the colors. Posterize generates a fairly recognizable effect and is valuable as a platform for other filters.

Image Adjust

► Levels ► Curves

► Brightness/ ► Color Balance
  Contrast

► Hue/Saturation ► Replace Color

► Selective Color ► Auto Levels

► Desaturate ► Variations

These filters aren't just image editing tools. Use Levels, Curves, Brightness/Contrast, and Lightness in the Hue/Saturation feature to manipulate the brightness and midtones of an image. Use Hue/Saturation, Color Balance, and Replace colors to edit the colors. Edit the individual color channel curves, use the Colorize feature in Hue/Saturation, or use Color Balance to condense the hues to a single color or a few groups of colors. Wild Curves, especially within individual channels, can generate interesting effects as well.

Modes

Manipulating the color palette of an indexed image via Color Table can produce interesting results, although it can also be time consuming. Blending colors within the Color Table is an easy way to reduce an image to a single color range. You can do this by clicking on the first color square and dragging down to the last. Photoshop will prompt you to choose the two colors that it will blend. To create interesting dithering patterns with indexed colors, reduce the texture to smaller bit depths and then convert it back to RGB. You can create interesting textures by creating various dithered versions of an image and then combining these versions with Layer modes.

Layer Modes

- Dissolve
- Multiply
- Screen
- Overlay
- Soft Light
- Hard Light
- Darken
- Lighten
- Difference
- Hue
- Saturation
- Color
- Luminosity

Some of the most interesting possibilities with texture combinations are possible via layers, layer modes, and opacity settings. Consult Photoshop's online help for a brief, yet comprehensive, description of each layer. Multiply, Screen, Overlay, Hard Light, Difference, and Luminosity tend to be the most handy modes for texture generation. Opacity can dull the effect of a combination, but it often leaves the image desaturated—a situation that can often be fixed with the Adjust tools.

Third-Party Texture Generation Programs

Currently, most of the better texture generation programs and plug-ins are only available on the Mac OS. Some textures can be borrowed from 3D applications by rendering them on a flat surface that fills up the image.

KPT Power Tools has become somewhat ubiquitous; however, a better gradient designer isn't available anywhere, and the Texture Explorer can be the basis for valuable textures as noted previously. KPT Power Tools 3 even generates attractive moving textures. KPT Convolver is based on the principle, described in this chapter, of mixing various effects. By combining various common effects such as reliefs, tints, and blurs, KPT Convolver can speed up the experimentation process. KPT Convolver lacks a noise feature, although it does have one of the best Gaussian Blur and Unsharp mask features in the industry.

Although Screen Caffeine Pro is not a texture generation program, it's a great example of the kind of engaging textures you can render in Photoshop. Jawai Interactive offers more than 600 highly attractive textures for multimedia and the web. These textures are built entirely from scratch within Photoshop. Of course, Metatools is well known for having some of the most attractive and entertaining interfaces in the industry.

Admittedly, generating textures from scratch can end up being very time consuming, but the more mastery you gain over the various possibilities, the more money and time you can save in the long run. Not everything can be done within Photoshop, but what can be done, can be done quickly and easily—after you know the techniques. Also, the time experimenting with creating textures from scratch can be lots of fun.

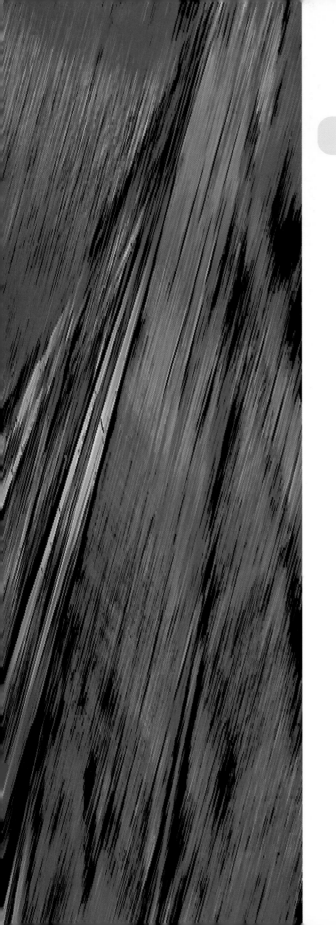

CHAPTER 4

The Beveled Look

Beveling is among the most ubiquitous looks utilized in multimedia and the web. Although common, beveling is actually a complex effect to accomplish in Photoshop and is one of the few effects that still rely as heavily on Channels as on Layers.

Covered in this chapter:

► Variations

► Button Up and Down States

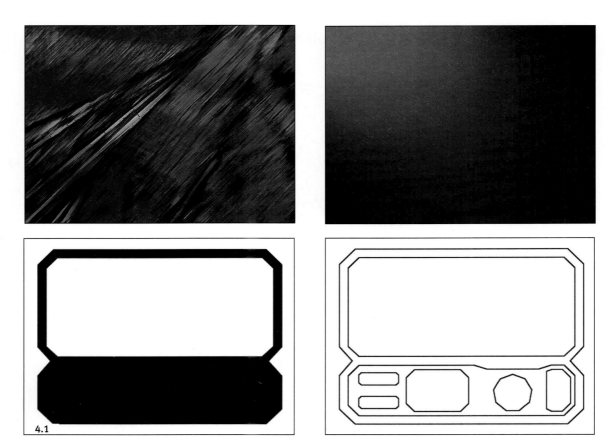

4.1

1. Begin with two textures or images on separate layers as shown in figure 4.1. Name the layers Background Texture and Interface Texture respectively. The Interface Texture layer should be on top of the Background Texture layer. The textures in this example were generated using the techniques covered in the last chapter.

2. Create a new channel called Skinny. Open a template for the interface from a scanned sketch, a basic shape built from within Photoshop, or from artwork generated in a vector-based application such as Illustrator, FreeHand, or CorelDRAW!, and cut and paste it into the new channel. After pasting, deselect by hitting Ctrl/Command+D.

   This template was created in CorelDRAW! and exported as a 72 dpi, RGB, TIFF. Templates from vector-based programs can be exported at exact size by centering a white box with no outline around the template and exporting the template with the box. For a 640×480 image, the box should be 8.889 inches wide by 6.667 inches high.

note

Note that this interface is generated from many pieces. The following steps cover the generation of the main plate for this interface. The rest of the interface is generated using these same steps.

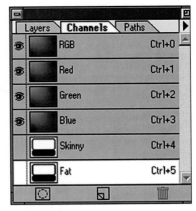

3. In the Channels palette create a new channel and name it Fat (see fig 4.2).

4. Drag the Skinny channel down to the lower left icon in the Channels palette to load the selection in the Fat channel.

5. Select Contract from the Select, Modify menu and enter a value of about 5 pixels and select OK. The smaller the value the thinner the bevel. The bigger the value the wider the bevel.

6. Select Fill from the Edit menu, fill the selection with white, and deselect.

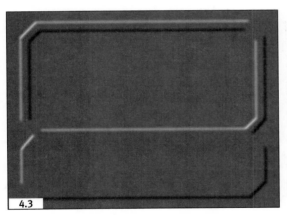
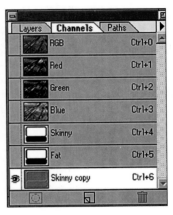

7. Drag the Skinny channel to the lower center icon in the Channels palette to duplicate the channel (see fig. 4.3).

8. Select Gaussian Blur from the Filter, Blur menu and enter a radius of about 3. This value is variable, but it needs to be wide enough to cover the bevel space that is the width entered in Step 5 (5 pixels).

9. Select Emboss from the Filter, Stylize menu and apply an emboss to the channel. The values used in the Emboss dialog box are highly variable. Enter a value of approximately 135 for the angle for an upper-left light source and approximately 45 for an upper-right light source. The Height and Amount settings polarize the emboss effect, so use low values for soft light and high values for hard light. This example used values of 138 for the angle, Height 6 pixels, and 150 for the Amount. For Bevels, higher Heights and Amounts are usually preferred so that the highlights and shadows show up clearly.

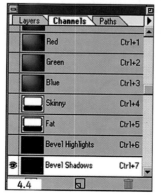

10. Drag the embossed Skinny Copy channel down to the center icon in the Channels palette to create a copy. Rename one of the copies Bevel Highlights and one of the copies Bevel Shadows (see fig. 4.4).

11. Select the Bevel Highlights channel and then select Levels (Ctrl+L) from the Image, Adjust menu.

12. Click on the black Eyedropper (the one on the left) and click anywhere within the 50% gray area in the channel. This converts all of the pixel values that are from 0–128 to black, leaving a channel that selects the highlighted areas.

13. Select the Bevel Shadows layer and then select Levels. Click on the white Eyedropper (the one on the right) and click anywhere within the 50% gray area in the channel. This converts all the pixel values that are from 129–256 to white.

14. Select invert from the Image, Map menu to create a selection for the shadows.

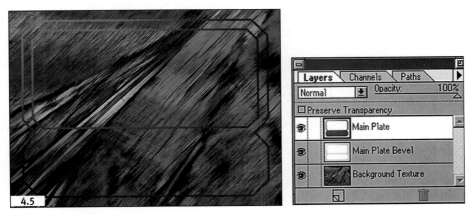

15. Open the Layers palette and drag the Interface Texture layer down to the lower left icon in the Layers palette to create a duplicate layer (see fig. 4.5).

16. Change the name of the Interface Texture copy layer to Main Plate and the Interface Texture layer to Main Plate Bevel. With the Main Plate Bevel layer selected, choose Load Selection from the Select menu.

17. Choose the Skinny channel and select the Invert check box. Select OK. Then choose Contract from the Select, Modify menu. Enter a value of 2 pixels in the Contract dialog box and select OK. Press Delete. A value of 2 pixels ensures that the layers will slightly overlap.

18. Choose Load Selection from the Select menu and load the Fat channel. Press Delete. Select the Main Plate layer, load the Skinny channel, and delete.

4.6

19. Select the Main Plate layer and Load the Bevel Highlights channel. Select the Brightness/Contrast (Ctrl+B) controls from the Image, Adjust menu and increase the brightness and contrast (see fig. 4.6).

20. Load the Bevel Shadows channel and use the Brightness/Contrast controls to decrease the brightness and contrast. Obviously the values used with the Brightness/Contrast controls are variable. Any filter can be applied within this selection to augment the highlights. Particularly valuable adjustments can be made with the Color Balance and Hue/Saturation controls. The highlights on the bevels in this image were enriched by adding a little yellow in the highlights and midtones. The shadows on the bevels were given some additional blue in the shadows and midtones with the Color Balance controls.

4.7

21. Add beveled elements using the same techniques in this exercise (see fig. 4.7). Dozens of layers can be used, but Photoshop is limited to only 16 channels. One method of getting around this is to save the file in stages and then delete older channels to make room for new ones. Interfaces tend to take up relatively little space on a hard drive, so save multiple versions as often as your resources allow.

4.8

22. You can easily add recessed areas by inverting the highlights and shadows in the bevels (see fig. 4.8). Notice also that the buttons (and any other surface) can be recessed by using the Button Bevel Highlights mask to create shadows and the Button Bevel Shadows mask to create highlights.

Intruder Alert

Recommend
Evasive
Action

4.9

23. Continue adding touches until the interface is complete (see fig. 4.9). Try to add some stylistic elements to the interface, such as screws and nuts, attractive highlights, shadows in non-functional parts of the interface, and unique lighting and design elements that add to the overall look of the interface. Too much style will distract the user from the main content, but too little style will leave the interface looking empty or shallow. It is often the intangible elements that set a design apart.

Variations

Variations to the interface.

By using a layer for every element, it is easy to make adjustments and experiment with variations (see fig 4.10). Backgrounds can be easily changed, lighting can be adjusted, and elements can be removed and then added again to observe their impact on the design as a whole. Figures 4.11 through 4.14 show some other variations that you can create.

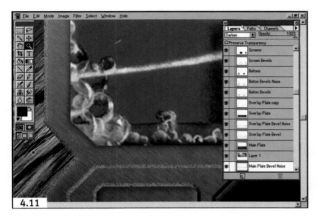

4.11

Noise applied to duplicate bevel layers with the Darken mode.

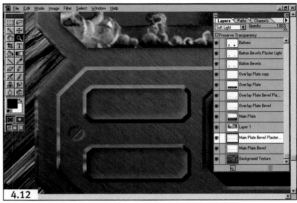

4.12

Adobe Gallery Effects' Plaster added to duplicate bevel layers with Soft Light. (Used with express permission. Adobe® and Image Club Graphics™ are trademarks of Adobe Systems Incorporated.)

4.13

KPT Texture Explorer 3.0 added to the surfaces layers with Soft Light.

4.14

Clouds added to the surfaces layers with Soft Light.

Quick and easy variations can also be achieved by duplicating a layer, adding effects to the duplicate layer, and then applying various layer modes. Soft Light is particularly valuable for adding unique lighting effects to bevels to help set them apart from the more common beveled look.

Thinner and thicker bevels can be created by decreasing or increasing the pixels in the Contract dialog box in step 2. The Modify options under the Select menu will only modify up to 16 pixels. For a very thick bevel either apply the Contract filter multiple times or build the Fat mask in your vector-based application.

By creating the bevels on separate layers, you have complete control over how they look. If the highlights are too bright, you can just change the highlights. If you want a different texture on the bevels, you can easily make the change. There are other methods for creating Bevels in Photoshop, but this one provides the most versatility.

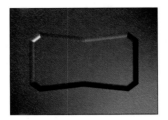

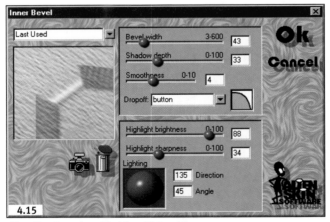

Creating bevels with Alien Skin software.

Alien Skin Software offers a filter, Black Box 2.0, that automates much of this process. Although Black Box 2.0 does not offer as much versatility as the above technique, it can quickly create beveled buttons, interfaces, and other elements with its unique flavor (see fig. 4.15). Black Box 2.0 comes with an inner and outer bevel. Several bevel styles can be applied, including "button" and "mesa."

Button Up and Down States

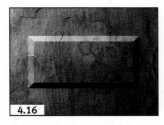

A button in its up and down states.

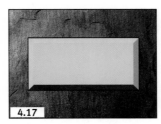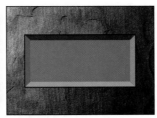

Different colors can indicate up and down states for buttons.

Button up and down states make a button look depressed (see fig. 4.16). The two states do not have to convey the appearance of depression. In some instances a different color might work as if the button were lit when pressed (see fig 4.17). Anything that indicates that a button has been pressed can work as a down state for a button. Up and down states for beveled buttons are easy to create. Simply by reversing the highlights and shadows, you can make the button appear to be depressed.

CHAPTER 5

The Embossed Look

Along with the beveled look, embossing (adding highlights and shadows to flat textures and images) is the main technique for adding depth and dimension to 2D artwork in Photoshop. Whether subtle or exaggerated, embossing emulates the look of 3D. As with most effects created in Photoshop, the embossed look can be accomplished in various ways—each of which produce unique characteristics.

Covered in this chapter:

► Calculated Emboss Method

► Quick Emboss Method

► Button Up and Down States

The first method demonstrated in this chapter provides the most control, allowing for highlights and shadows to be manipulated separately. This method gives you the most freedom to create unique characteristics on your interfaces. The alternative method is quicker, but less flexible, and is handy to know when versatility is not a requirement.

Almost any surface can be made to look three-dimensional merely by skillful positioning of highlights and shadows. Embossing creates the effect of a raised or 3D surface by adding highlights and shadows to a surface. Embossing has become a popular effect because it is an easy way to add dimension to images that appear on a flat (or slightly concave) monitor. Interfaces with dimension can often be more appealing and intuitive because they emulate reality more closely than flat images. Embossing provides among the easiest ways to achieve dimension.

Calculated Emboss Method

The Calculated Emboss method provides the most control over the embossing effect. It enables you to precisely control and edit the highlights and shadows that will appear in your finished artwork. By building the highlights and shadows on separate layers, you can combine multiple versions of the highlights or shadows layers to augment the effect or adjust the opacity to reduce the effect. Although this method takes a little more time, the complete control over the final effect is always worth it.

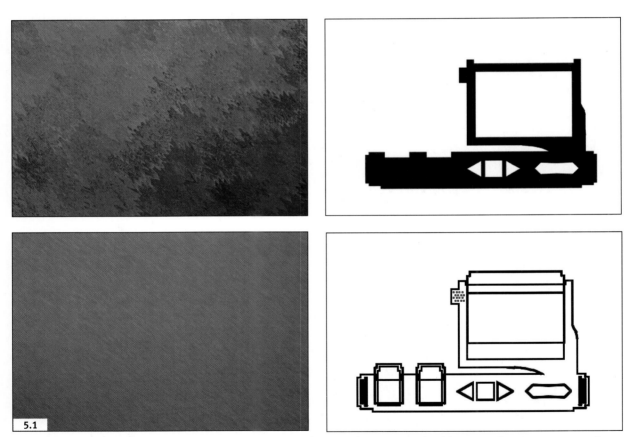

5.1

1. Begin with two textures or images on separate layers. The textures in this example were generated using the techniques covered in Chapter 3, "Textures from Scratch." Name the layers Background Texture and Interface Texture, respectively. Position the Interface Texture layer above the Background Texture layer.

INTERFACE DESIGN with Photoshop

Create a new layer called Template. Open a template for the interface from a scanned sketch, from a basic shape built within Photoshop, or from artwork generated in a vector-based application—such as Illustrator, FreeHand, or CorelDRAW!—and cut and paste it into the new layer. This template was created in CorelDRAW! and exported as a 72 dpi, RGB TIFF.

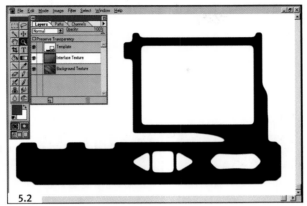

5.2

2. Click on the Template layer in the Layers palette and apply a Gaussian Blur to it. The Gaussian Blur setting depends on the desired intensity of the effect. The more you blur, the more the Levels filter will have to work with. This example uses a setting of 4.5.

3. Next, select Levels from the Image, Adjust menu (Ctrl+L). Remember that the values for Levels are somewhat subjective. The key is to collapse the mid-range of the blend from black to white around the edges of the interface without causing aliasing. To do this, drag the black-and-white triangles, or enter new values for the Input levels so that the levels are closer to one another—but not too close. Levels in the low range will result in a fatter interface whereas levels in the high range will contract the interface. For this example, values of 65, 1.00, and 95 were entered into the Input levels from left to right.

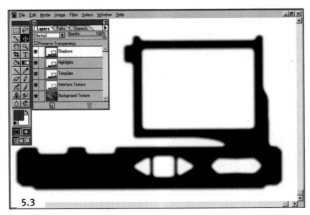

5.3

4. With the Template layer still selected, open the Channels palette. Drag the RGB channel in the Channels palette down to the channel icon to create a selection. Choose Save Selection from the Select menu to save the selection as a channel.

Go back to the Layers palette and with the Interface Texture layer selected, press Delete to make the white areas transparent. Next, select the Template layer and delete. Select None from the Select menu (Ctrl+D) to deselect.

Reselect the Template layer and drag it down to the Layer icon in the Layers palette to create a new layer; name the new layer Highlights. Apply a Gaussian Blur to the Highlights layer. The more blur that is applied, the more the highlights and shadows appear. Use a radius of 3 for this example.

Drag and drop the Highlights layer onto the Layer icon and rename the Highlights copy layer Shadows. Select the Shadows layer and nudge it up and to the left four times in each direction. Select the Highlights layer and nudge it down and to the right four times in each direction.

> **note**
>
> Photoshop enables you to use the arrow keys to nudge layers or selections one pixel at a time. If you have the Marquee tool selected, pressing the arrow keys will nudge a selection. If you have the Move tool selected, pressing the arrow keys will nudge a layer.

5.4

5. Select Calculations from the Image menu. Under Source 1, select Template in the Layer box and Transparency in the Channel box, and make sure the Invert option is checked. Under Source 2, select Shadows in the Layer box and Transparency in the Channel box, and leave the Invert option unchecked. Under Blending, select Add and set Opacity at 100%. Under Result, make sure the file you are working on is selected (as opposed to New) and select New in the Channel box (see figure 5.5). Doing so will create a new channel (#5) for the shadows area.

Open the Channels palette and invert the new channel by pressing Ctrl+I. Select the Shadows layer, choose Select All from the Select menu (Ctrl+A), and press Delete. Choose Load Selection from the Select menu, and then load channel #5. Select Fill from the Edit menu and fill the Shadows layer 100% black.

5.5

Repeat this process for the Highlights layer using the Highlights layer in the Layer box under Source 2. The Highlights calculation will generate channel #6.

After generating channel #6, choose the Highlights layer, Select All, Delete, and use the inverted selection from channel #6 to fill the white (the background color by default). To delete the Template layer, drag it to the Trash Can icon.

> **tip**
>
> The method just described is the best way to generate the highlight and shadows masks if you want to clearly see what's happening while it's happening. However, if you do not prefer to delete the white space from the Template layer as discussed in Step 4 (transparency increases file size in Photoshop), you can use the Multiply mode and the Gray channels instead of the Add mode and the Transparency channels when using Calculations to build the channels.

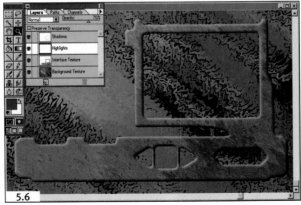

5.6

6. If the Interface texture is not below the Highlights and Shadows layers, drag it down below them. Now if you view all of the layers you will see that the Highlights and Shadows layers create an embossed look to the interface. You can adjust the highlights and shadows independently by adjusting the opacity on the Highlights and Shadows layers. In addition, you also have the selections that

you can use now or later to add color to the highlights and shadows, such as yellows and oranges for highlights and blues and purples for shadows.

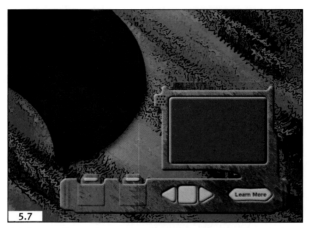

Adding various elements to complete the interface.

You can continue adding elements using the Emboss technique until the design is complete. Although this method is among the more involved approaches to the embossed look, its versatility often makes it preferable. Of course, if you would rather make the adjustments to the main layer using the channels without adding layers for the highlights and shadows, you will have to redo that layer if you need to change the texture or make other drastic edits.

Importing the video screen and function bars into the interface.

Keeping various interface elements on separate layers also helps when you need to make the interface actually function. In this example, the video screen and function bars are each on separate layers, making it easy to export them as separate units so that they can be reintegrated in an authoring program (such as Macromedia Director) and programmed to move independently.

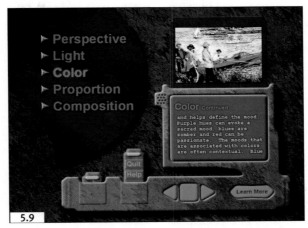

Editing the interface by changing its background and image.

As mentioned in Chapter 1, "Interface Design," building an interface using multiple layers also makes tweaking, editing, and variations easier to do (see fig. 5.9).

> **tip**
>
> Some interfaces may require dozens of layers and channels. Keeping all these layers and objects on file can be tedious, but rebuilding the channels and layers several times can be even more tedious. An effective method for dealing with this problem is to save a separate file that acts as a repository for channels and layers. Channels and layers can be easily dragged and dropped between files as needed.

Quick Emboss Method

Although much less versatile than the Calculated Emboss method, the Quick Emboss method for embossing can come in handy for either prototyping or when its effect is sufficient without alteration. This method does not enable you to adjust the opacity for highlights and shadows, but it does create a clean embossed look for projects that don't require the precision of the Calculated method.

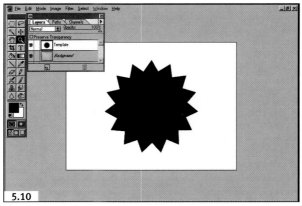

5.10

1. Begin with a background texture or image. Either import a template or create a shape for a button or interface on a new layer.

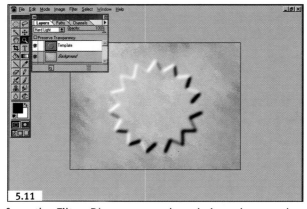

5.11

2. Select Gaussian Blur from the Filter, Blur menu and apply it to the template layer. Again, the more the blur, the more potential the emboss effect will have. Select Emboss from the Filter, Stylize menu and emboss the template layer. Select Hard Light as the mode in the layers palette.

tip

To create a mask for editing the embossed area, copy the template or artwork layer and create a channel out of it before applying Gaussian Blur. Decide upon the amount of Gaussian Blur you are going to apply. Expand the channel one half of the amount you are going to Gaussian Blur by loading the channel onto itself (drag template channel to the lower left icon in Channels palette), inverting the selection, and choosing Expand from the Select Modify menu (assuming the template/artwork is black surrounded by white).

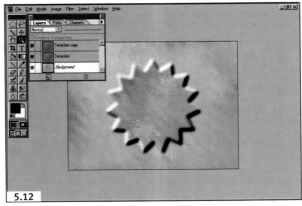

5.12

3. To decrease the amount of the highlight or shadow effect, lower the opacity of the template layer. To increase the amount of the highlight or shadow effect, drag and drop the embossed layer down to the lower left icon in the Layers palette, creating a duplicate layer. Duplicate layers increase the effect of their original layer. Edit the embossed area with the optional mask. You can create similar effects with the Overlay, Soft Light, and Luminosity modes.

Beyond the inability to edit highlights and shadows independently with this method, this method isn't always handy when adding quick embosses to layers because it can leave unwanted residual gray pixels. If, for example, a layer (layer A) does not take up the entire image size or space, the 50% gray area of the quick emboss layer (layer B) will be added to layer A when the two layers are merged on any spots that are transparent on layer A. Therefore, layer B must be transparent in the same areas that layer A is to avoid any unwanted gray pixels.

Button Up and Down States

The emboss effect is classically used for buttons. Often in multimedia, you want to make a button look like it has been pressed or depressed when it is clicked on to emulate reality. This is referred to as button up and down states. When a button is in its normal embossed state, it is in its *up state*. When a button has been clicked on, it may temporarily change (either until the user lets up on the mouse button or until the button is clicked again) to a depressed state, which is referred to as its *down state*.

As with the beveled effect, inverting the highlights and shadows is a simple method for creating a down state for the embossed. Do not bother to rebuild the layers; simply select Invert from the Image, Map menu to invert the Highlights and Shadows layers. Altering the color can highlight the down state even further.

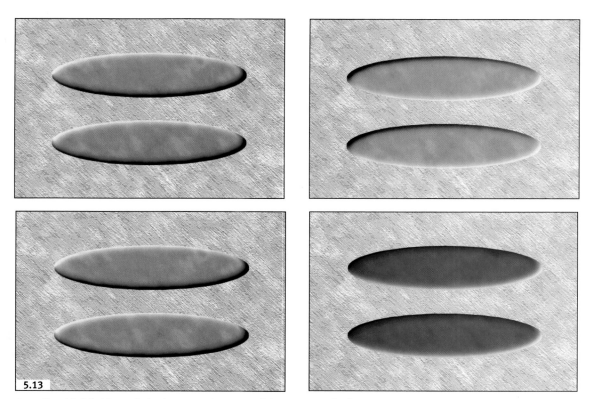

5.13

Inverting highlights and shadows creates up and down states for buttons.

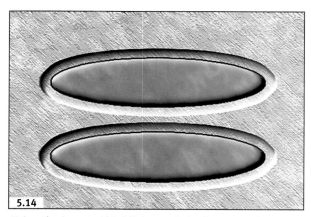

5.14

Using the inverted highlights and shadows can also create a recessed effect on the background.

Embossing emulates the look of 3D. Photoshop enables you to use a variety of techniques to generate the embossed look, including the Calculated Emboss method and the Quick Emboss method. The Calculated method allows for more flexibility in editing and creating new layers, whereas the Quick method is best used for fast, simple embosses.

CHAPTER 6

Shadows, Glows, and Other Bread and Butter Techniques

D rop shadows, glows, and other related effects are as useful as they are ubiquitous. As with any simple technique, these techniques can be used to create effective design or visual night-mares. Effective use of lighting, glows, transparency, and cutout effects can set interface design apart. In general, the key is to use the effects without calling attention to them, except when it is appropriate, such as using a glow to call attention to a button.

Covered in this chapter:

- ► Basic Shadow

- ► Basic Glow

- ► Basic Transparency

- ► Basic Cutouts

Basic Shadow

Shadows are one of the most basic cues the human eye uses to interpret depth in space. When light is obstructed by an object, the object casts a shadow. Casting shadows is easy with Photoshop, especially with the introduction of Layers in version 3, that it has long been one of the most popular methods for adding depth and dimension to Photoshop imagery. Often the trick to shadows is not in their creation, but in making them realistic and attractive.

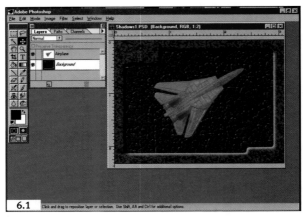

After an object is on its own layer, it is easy to create a drop shadow of it. In this example a background was created with textures from Screen Caffeine Pro and the airplane (and the tank that you will use later) was masked and then cut and pasted as separate layers over the background from Metatool's Power Photos.

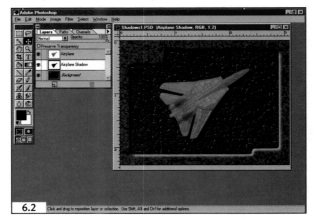

1. This discussion presumes that you are starting with two layers: a Background layer and an Object layer. The assumption is that the Object layer has had all pixels not within the object deleted (and thus made transparent). To create the shadow of the object, drag it to the New Layer icon in the Layers

INTERFACE DESIGN with Photoshop

palette, rename the new layer Airplane (or whatever your object is) Shadow, and drag the Shadow layer below the original object layer. With the Shadow layer selected, choose Fill from the Edit menu, making sure Preserve Transparency is selected, and fill the object with black. Select the Move tool and either move or nudge the Shadow layer down and to the right of the Airplane layer. Positioning the shadow to the lower right presumes that the light source is from the upper left. If the light source were from the upper right, you would want to position the shadow to the lower left.

Light travels in a straight line unless it is otherwise redirected by mirrors or other methods. Typically digital images limit themselves to one light source to simplify the shadow structure and avoid confusing viewers. If you have a light source at the upper left, upper right, and lower center, the shadows might be difficult to both render and visually interpret. Multiple light sources are usually best left to 3D programs that are capable of accurately rendering multiple light sources.

The shadow in this example is a hard shadow. Hard shadows indicate that the object is not very far from its background. Most shadows have some amount of gradation to them even when they are very close to the object from which they are being cast.

6.3

2. To soften the shadow, add Gaussian Blur. The amount of the Gaussian Blur depends upon the desired effect. The shadow for the airplane on the right was blurred with a radius of 10, and the shadow for the airplane on the left was blurred with a radius of 40. The more distance between an object and the background on which the shadow is cast, the more the shadow diffuses. The shadow on the right has a smaller setting and is closer to the subject, making it look lower to the ground. The shadow on the left has a larger setting and is further away from the subject, creating the illusion that the airplane on the left is higher. Incidentally, the fact that the airplane on the left overlaps the border also aids in the perception that it is higher.

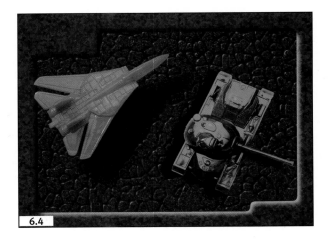

6.4

As previously indicated, the shadows should make sense. Many users might not even notice why the image in figure 6.4 disturbs them. Although multiple light sources are not uncommon in reality, interfaces generally work best with one light source. This image disturbs not only because the shadows are in opposite directions, but because the tank has a brighter light source than the airplane. In theory, the airplane might be believable with a brighter light source because it appears to be higher and therefore closer to the light source, but as it is, the image is completely illogical.

Dressing Up Shadows

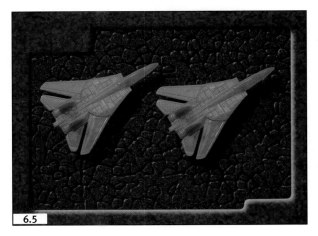

6.5

You can vary the shadow by decreasing the opacity of the shadow or by filling the shadow layer with a dark color instead of black. The airplane on the left has a shadow with a 60% opacity setting, and the shadow on the right was filled with a dark green color. Also try using many of the Adjust features, such as Curves, Levels, and Hue/Saturation to enrich your shadows.

The Gaussian Blur filter creates a fat shadow. That is, Gaussian Blur spreads the blur both inside and outside the original object. This effect can be as desirable as it is problematic. If it does become a problem, you can decrease the contrast and the shape of the shadow in steps after converting it to black (or a dark color) with the Maximum filter (Filter, Offset). Use a Maximum radius value that is approximately half of the intended Gaussian Blur radius value.

Basic Glow

6.6

Glows are almost the inverse of shadows in terms of implementing them in Photoshop. Instead of filling the duplicate layer—which should be named Glow—of the object with black, you fill it with bright colors such as yellow and white. (You do not have to use bright colors with this technique.) Again, because Gaussian Blur spreads the blur both inside and outside the original object, and glows often emanate in all directions from the subject, it is often desirable to spread out the base of pixels used for the glow. To do this, fill the duplicate layer with black as in Step 1 of the shadows technique. Then use the Minimum filter (Filter, Offset) to spread out the pixels. Use a Minimum radius value that is up to as much as the intended Gaussian Blur radius value. After spreading out the base, fill the Glow layer with the desired color.

Decrease the effect by reducing the opacity of the Glow layer, or increase the effect by creating a duplicate Glow layer. The example in figure 6.6 utilized a duplicate Glow layer to brighten the glow effect.

Glow Effects

6.7

Interesting effects can also be created by applying various filters and using various modes with duplicate Glow layers. In the previous example, several duplicate layers were created. The Twirl filter was used on two layers. One was placed on top of the light bulb and one beneath. Then the top layer had its bottom half cut, and the bottom layer had its top layer cut. Noise was applied to a third layer, and the Dust & Scratches filter was used to polarize the noise. Then the Overlay mode was used to create a somewhat electrified effect. Again, also try using many of the Adjust features, such as Curves, Levels and Hue/Saturation to enrich your glows.

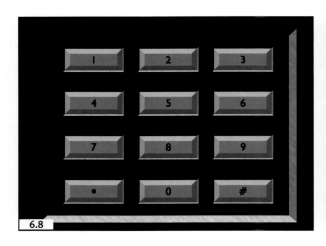

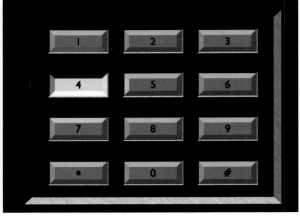

6.8

Glows are effective for button up and down effects. In this example, the button turns yellow when depressed. Glows were added to the surrounding surfaces. This bevel effect was generated by creating templates in a vector-based program for each series of bevels. Each template was loaded as a selection and the Brightness/Contrast filter was used to create the highlights and shadows. A separate duplicate layer of the buttons was then created for each button, and selections were used to delete all the areas except the main button (button 4) and the surfaces on which the glows would be cast. The surfaces were selected apart from the button and then blurred, and the button was selected apart from the surfaces and inverted. Then the yellow hue was added with Hue/Saturation. See Chapter 13, "Sliders, Dials, Switches, Doodads, and Widgets," for a closer look at creating bevel effects from vector-based templates.

In a multimedia title, each button down state would have to be generated separately. Because each button is the same, however, one button down state can be generated, and then the individual numbers added separately to save time.

Basic Transparency

Transparency is a characteristic of many materials, such as glass, some plastics, and crystals. Transparency is another subtle way of achieving the visual perception of depth in an image. If something can be seen through an object, the eye automatically interprets a certain amount of space to account for the transparent object and the object that is seen through it. Once again, achieving transparency in Photoshop is easy, but making it realistic and attractive requires a little extra work.

6.9

Transparency is achieved by adjusting the opacity of objects. This figure utilizes the bevel effect from Chapter 4, "The Beveled Look." A simple video screen was created by applying the effect to a solid color and then adjusting the layers to 65% opacity.

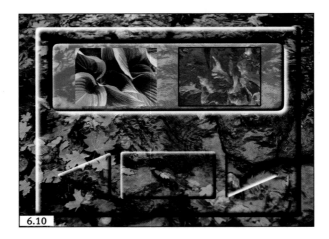

6.10

An alternative approach to transparency can be achieved by using the embossed look from Chapter 5, "The Embossed Look," without a main body to the interface. In other words, by using only the highlights and shadows for the emboss technique, the interface can be made to look transparent.

6.11

Transparency effects don't have to be used specifically to create interface elements. The glare on the stylized TV set (created with images from Classic PIO and Photo Disc), for instance, was generated by importing the shape from CorelDRAW! as a channel, blurring it, loading it as a selection on a new layer, and then filling the selection with white. With the stroke on a separate layer, it becomes easy to adjust the intensity of the glare with the opacity slider. Similarly, the shading on the background of this file was generated by creating channels with simple diagonal linear gradients, one for the upper right corner and one for the lower left. After the layers were filled with black using the channel selections, the shadows were adjusted with the opacity settings. Although both of these effects could have been implemented with other methods, using layers provided much more flexibility and control.

Basic Cutouts

Cutouts are a matter of making a selection on a layer and deleting it to show the layer or background below. Although easy, the cutout is an integral technique for interface design. The next section shows you how to create a sliding panel using the cutout technique.

Using Cutouts to Create a Sliding Panel

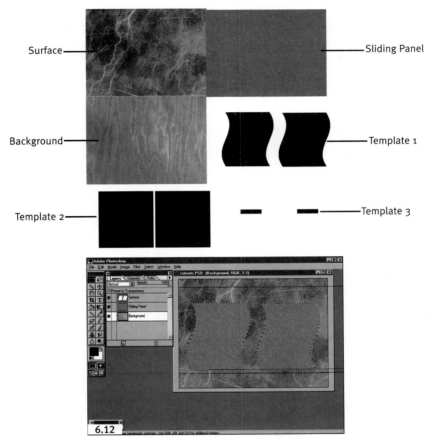

1. The trick in dealing with the cutout effect is dealing with the shadows. Begin with separate layers for the background, the sliding panel, and the surface. This example was generated from two textures from Image Club for the background and surface and a texture generated with techniques from Chapter 3, "Textures from Scratch." Name the top layer Surface and middle layer Sliding Panel. A separate texture was used for each layer to help differentiate the layers, but that is obviously not a requirement. Cut and paste templates or generate masks in the Channels palette for the cutouts, the sliding panels, and any additional design elements. Load the cutout selection on the surface layer and select delete.

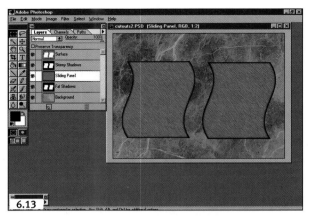

6.13

2. Invert the selection used for the cutout to create two new layers named Skinny Shadows and Fat Shadows, and fill them both with black, invert the selection, and delete on both layers. Move the Skinny Shadows layer below the Surface layer but above the Sliding Panel layer. Move the Fat Shadows layer below the Sliding Panel layer. With the Skinny Shadows layer selected, apply the Minimum filter (Filter, Other) with a small radius (4 was used for this example). Apply an equal radius setting with the Gaussian Blur filter (Filter, Blur). The higher the Minimum and Gaussian Blur settings, the more recessed the sliding panel appears to be from the surface. Now apply the Minimum filter to the Fat Shadows layer with a setting of approximately three times the Skinny Shadows setting (you may have to do multiple applications of the Minimum filter because its maximum setting is 10). Next, with the Fat Shadows layer still selected, apply the Gaussian Blur filter with a radius setting of approximately two times the Minimum filter radius for the Fat Shadows layer.

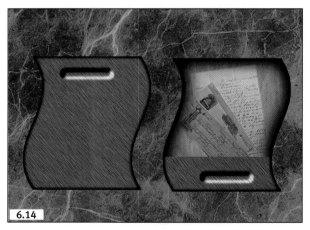

6.14

3. Load the sliding panel selection and delete. Add any design elements. In this example, two panels were created so that one could be shown drawn back. Notice that the open sliding panel shows two levels of shadows. A slight shadow is cast on the panel, and when the panel is open, a different shadow is cast on the background. Because the Skinny Shadows layer is smaller, it gets lost within the Fat Shadows when the sliding panel is open. Notice also that any objects, such as the documents (courtesy of CMCD) from this example, should be placed below the Fat Shadow. Finally, notice that these "shadows" are in effect dark glows—they have not been offset at all. Offset shadows can also be created by deleting the parts of the shadow or glow that you don't want.

Although shadows, glows, transparency, and cutout effects are simple, they are integral to interface design and web imagery. All these effects are commonly used for easy text effects and are constantly used in conjunction with one another for creating even the most complex interfaces. By generating these effects on separate layers, it becomes easy to tweak as much as a deadline allows and also allows for more opportunity to get the effect just right.

PART II

Advanced and Specialized Topics

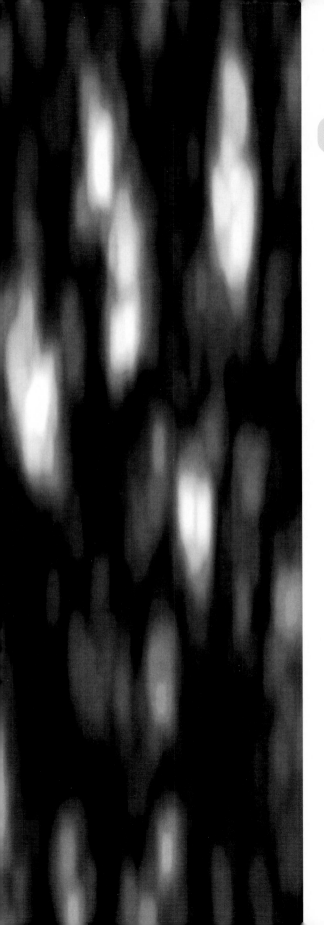

CHAPTER 7

The Look of Chrome, Glass, and Plastic

Many interface metaphors lend themselves to common materials. Because most real-world interfaces are made with metal, plastic, and glass, Photoshop is often called upon to generate these special effects. Fortunately, Photoshop is capable of creating these effects largely from scratch.

Covered in this chapter:

- ► The Chrome/Metal Look

- ► The Glass/Crystal Look

- ► The Plastic/Gel Look

The Chrome/Metal Look

Chromes and metals are common in futuristic themes. Science fiction has established the look of shiny metals as part of the metaphor that defines it. Other themes lend themselves to the look of metal. An interface for a multimedia kiosk that educates viewers on metal alloys and their uses, for instance, would obviously lend itself to a metallic theme. Fortunately, metal effects are easy to create in Photoshop.

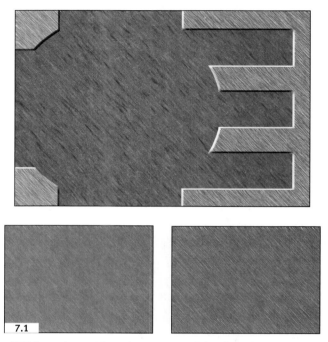

KPT Convolver adds a nice amount of depth to the brushed metal effect. Note the distortion at the edges of the bottom two examples.

Chapter 3, "Textures from Scratch," demonstrates an easy method for generating metal textures by adding a monochromatic noise to a gray page or selection and then applying Motion Blur. If the gray is light, you can add some contrast with Brightness/Contrast (Image, Adjust) after applying Motion Blur to add some detail. You can use an Emboss filter such as Aldus Gallery Effects' Emboss or KPT Convolver's Relief controls to add some depth. You can also use Photoshop's Emboss filter with extreme settings for a rough metal look. Applying Motion Blur often distorts the edges of the texture. To avoid this, create the texture in a separate larger file, paste the texture into the main file as a layer, and position the texture so that the distortions do not show.

1. To create a Chrome effect, begin with a basic black-and-white template on a separate layer and name the layer something such as Interface.

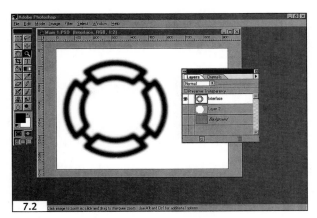

7.2

2. The template should be created so that the interface is black and the surrounding areas are white. This interface was created by importing a template from CorelDRAW!. The template was Gaussian Blurred and then the midtones were collapsed with Levels, as shown in Chapter 3.

3. Create a new channel from the template and name it Template Channel. Apply Gaussian Blur. The Gaussian Blur should be fairly substantial. A setting of 7.5 was used for this example (Note: These examples were produced at 300 ppi).

4. Drag the Interface layer down to the layer icon to create a duplicate layer.

5. Select the Move tool and nudge the duplicate up and to the left two times with the arrow keys. Select the original Interface layer and nudge it down and to the right two times with the arrow keys.

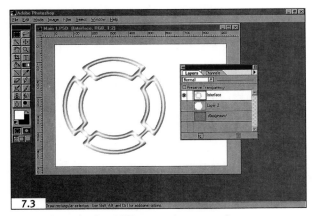

7.3

6. Select the duplicate layer and apply the Difference layer mode.

7. Merge the Interface layer and its duplicate by making only these layers visible and then selecting Merge Layers from the Layer palette pop-up menu.

8. Invert the image (Ctrl/Command+I). Load the Template channel, invert the selection, fill the selection with white, and deselect.

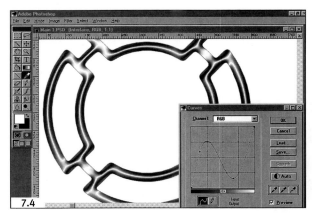

7.4

9. Open the Curves dialog box (Ctrl/Command +M). Adjust the curves to redistribute the tones in the template. By pulling dark gray tones up to white or light gray and light gray tones down to dark gray or black, you can create an effect similar to Chrome. This relatively basic curve generates a fairly conservative effect. We will cover some variations later.

7.5

10. After adjusting the curves to achieve the desired chrome effect, load the Template channel, invert the selection, delete, and then deselect.

11. Drag the Interface layer down to the new layer icon and rename the duplicate layer Interface Shadow.

12. Fill the Interface Shadow layer with black using the Edit, Fill command with Preserve Transparency checked.

13. Apply a Gaussian Blur and offset the shadow by nudging it or moving it with the Move tool.

14. Drag the Interface Shadow layer below the Interface layer in the Layers palette.

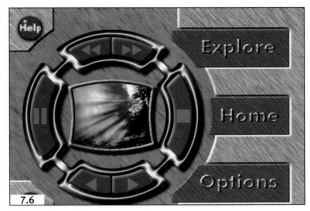

15. Add the rest of the interface elements.

This example was generated with techniques from Chapters 3–6 using an image from the Corel Professional Photos CD-ROM. The Chrome effect draws the eye more because of its wild appearance. It is a good idea to use Chrome sparingly and on elements that you want the user's eye to be drawn to.

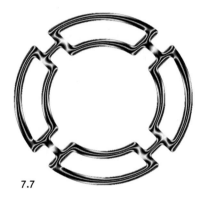

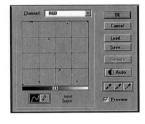

Wilder Chrome effects can be generated with curves.

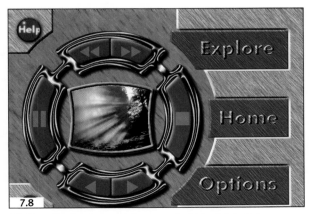

Fix the aliasing by applying a 1 pixel black border.

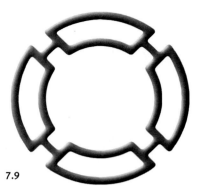

7.9

Create a variant substructure for the chrome effect with emboss.

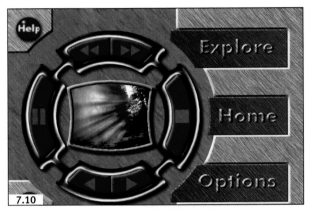

7.10

A subtle variation created with the Emboss substructure using a conservative curve manipulation similar to the first example.

The more gyrations on the Curve within the Curves dialog box the more unnatural the effect will look, and too many gyrations will cause aliasing. To remove the aliasing around the border, load the Template channel. Choose Contract from the Select, Modify menu and contract the selection 1 pixel. Invert the selection, fill with black, and deselect. Load the Template channel again, invert the selection, and delete. These steps replace the aliased borders with a 1 pixel black border.

Subtle variations of the Chrome effect can also be created from alternative bases.

1. For example, select New Layer from the Layers palette pop-up menu and fill the layer with white.

2. Load the Template channel, fill it with black, and deselect.

3. Apply a Gaussian Blur with a fairly substantial radius and then select Emboss from the Filter, Stylize menu. Photoshop's Emboss filter provides a wide range of possibilities—try various Angles, Heights and Amounts.

4. Load the Template channel, invert the selection, fill with white, and deselect.

5. Replace any aliased borders with a 1 pixel black border as discussed in the previous example.

Using this variation of the base as the substructure for the Curve manipulations can yield slightly different results from the original base. See Chapter 9, "Combinations and Unique Variations," for more ideas on how to generate other variations for the substructure for the curve manipulations.

7.11

A quick glass variation can be generated with the Chrome look using Screen mode on a duplicate layer filled with another color.

The Glass/Crystal Look

Glass and Crystalline effects utilize some of the techniques used to create Chrome effects. In fact, simply by creating a duplicate layer of the Interface layer from the previous Chrome technique, dragging it below the original copy, filling it with a color, and applying the Screen mode to the original Interface layer, you can create an easy Glass look. Glass and crystal interfaces are commonly used for otherworldly interfaces. They connote an almost utopian feeling of purity. Of course, glass and crystal are commonly used for interface elements that require transparency, such as the glass on video displays or thermometer-style meters. Glass and crystal interfaces lend themselves to themes. For example, a web site dedicated to glass blowing techniques might be an appropriate context for a glass interface.

7.12

Merge to layers that have had Difference Clouds applied to them using the Difference layer mode.

Unlike Metals, glass and crystalline objects are not opaque. In addition, some glass and most crystal objects have flaws within them that cause the highlights and shadows to displace. An easy way to create these flaws is with Difference Clouds (Filters, Render). The following discussion on glass and crystalline effects utilizes a new sample interface that was generated with the same techniques as shown in the chrome effect technique demonstrated previously.

1. After you have the basic interface constructed complete with the Template channel, create two new layers and fill them with white. Press D to ensure that foreground and background colors are set to the default black and white.

2. Apply Difference Clouds to both new layers.

3. Apply the Difference mode to the topmost Difference Cloud layer, merge the two layers, and name the new layer Flaw Map. The Difference Clouds filter creates a random effect, so your file may not look like the previous example.

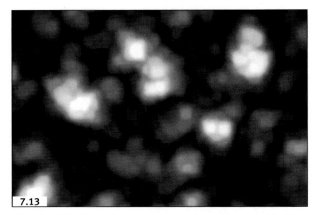

7.13

4. Apply a Gaussian Blur to the Flaw Map layer with a radius up to 5. At this point you can go several directions to prepare the Flaw Map. Basically, you are trying to make the flaw map look crystalline or at least to generate a balance between random contrast and a smooth gradation between the highlights and shadows of the flaw map.

5. Use the Maximum, Minimum, Median, Curves, Levels, and Contrast (within the Brightness/ Contrast feature) filters to achieve this balance. If there are too many dark areas, you can use Maximum, Levels, and Curves to increase the highlights of the Flaw Map. If there are too many light areas, use Minimum, Levels, and Curves to increase the shadows.

6. Adjust the contrast with the Brightness/ Contrast feature and use Median blend tonal borders to create a crystalline appearance. For this example, Maximum was used to spread out the highlights, a slight amount of contrast was applied, and then Median was used to crystallize the look a little.

Before using the Flaw Map.

After using the Flaw Map.

7. When the Flaw Map is ready, load the Template channel and delete. Make sure the Flaw Map layer is above the rest of the layers that make up the interface.

8. Apply the Soft Light Mode to the Flaw Map Layer. Reduce the opacity of the Flaw Map layer if the effect is too overbearing. In this example, the opacity was reduced to 80%. This interface was generated using images from the Corel Professional Photos CD-ROM.

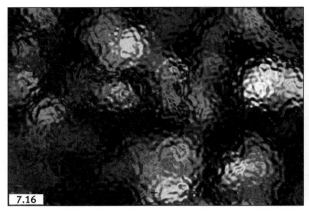
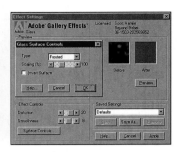

7.16

Adobe Gallery Effects' Glass filter can generate attractive flaw maps. (Used with express permission. Adobe® and Image Club Graphics™ are trademarks of Adobe Systems Incorporated.)

7.17

Adobe Gallery Effects' Glass flaw map applied to the interface. (Used with express permission. Adobe® and Image Club Graphics™ are trademarks of Adobe Systems Incorporated.)

An alternative to creating your own glass image is Adobe Gallery Effects' Glass filter, which also provides a nice Flaw Map texture. Apply the Glass filter to a Flaw Map created using the previous techniques. The Adobe Gallery Effects' Glass filter requires some sort of texture to work with to get a visible effect. Try distortions that are up toward the maximum (20) and Smoothness at approximately 6–12 in the Adobe Gallery Effects Glass Filter dialog box.

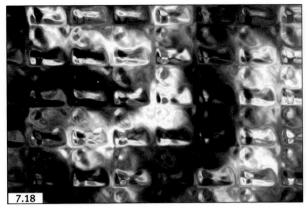

Adobe Gallery Effects' Glass filter using the Blocks Surface Controls. (Used with express permission. Adobe® and Image Club Graphics™ are trademarks of Adobe Systems Incorporated.)

Adobe Gallery Effects' Glass filter comes with several excellent Surface Control variations; you can load your own file to use as a map for the Glass filter.

Alien Skin Black Box 2.0 has a Glass filter that is perfect for generating flaw maps.

Alien Skin Black Box 2.0's Glass filter can also be used to make an excellent flaw map. Alien Skin's Glass filter effect works best for a flaw map on an oversized page because it applies a bevel around its edges. Create a new document that's about 60 pixels taller and wider than your interface's file size. Apply the Alien Skin Glass filter with a bevel width less than 30 pixels, Flaw Spacing 35–50, and Flaw Thickness about 75. Use an Opacity of about 15 and Refraction of about 50.

Use the Alien Skin Glass texture as a Flaw Map layer.

After applying the Alien Skin Glass filter, select Canvas Size from the Image menu, make sure the Placement square is in the center within the Canvas Size Dialog box, and resize the file to the same size as your interface file. Cut and paste the file as a new Flaw Map layer. Load the Template channel as a selection and delete. Use the Soft Light layer mode as discussed previously.

This example is shown with the interface layers deleted to better show the portions of the removed shadows.

Glass and crystalline objects are often at least somewhat transparent. Needless to say, it's easy to make an object transparent by reducing its opacity. However, if there's a drop shadow layer below the interface, it will show through. To remedy this, use the Template channel to delete the shadows from beneath the interface so that the underlying background texture can show through the interface. There may be instances where it may look better with the shadows left as they are, particularly when the interface is between 30–60 percent transparent, in which case a shadow may be, in reality, more visible. Interfaces that are very transparent (for example, 80-100 percent transparent) tend to cast less of a shadow.

The Plastic/Gel Look

Plastics can be both transparent and opaque, but they tend to be more on the opaque side. Opaque plastic surfaces tend to be solid colors and have fairly regular highlights and shadows. Transparent plastic objects tend be less shiny than glass objects because it is difficult to create plastic objects that are as clearly transparent as glass objects. For the purposes of this discussion, plastics are opaque and gels are transparent. Plastic interfaces are probably the most common, because plastic is so cheap in the real world. Most real-world interfaces—such as televisions, VCRs, microwaves, and so on—are made from plastic. Plastics and gels can be appropriately used in just about any genre because they are such ubiquitous materials.

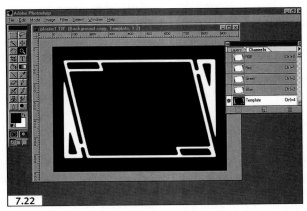

7.22

1. Begin with a basic template on a new layer. The area for the template should be black and the surrounding area should be white. Select all, copy, and paste into a new channel named Template. Then invert (Ctrl/Command+I).

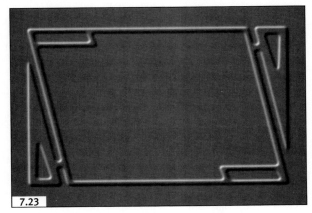

7.23

2. Create a new layer and fill it with white. Load the Template channel, fill with black, and deselect.

3. Apply a Gaussian Blur from 1.5–3.5 radius. Apply Photoshop's Emboss filter with a Height of 2–3 and Amount of 250–350.

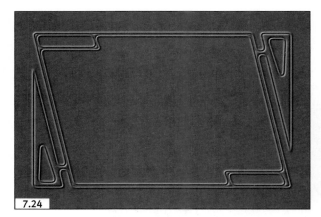

7.24

4. Create a new layer and fill it with white. Load the Template channel, fill it with black, and deselect.

5. Select the Maximum filter and apply with a radius of 3–5. This is a critical step. Try various Maximum settings for different effects.

6. Apply a Gaussian Blur similar to the one applied in the previous step.

7. Use Curves to apply a curve similar to the one shown in figure 7.24. Try other curves for various effects.

8. Apply Photoshop's Emboss filter with a Height of 2–3 and Amount of 75–150. Ensure that this layer is above the layer created in the previous step.

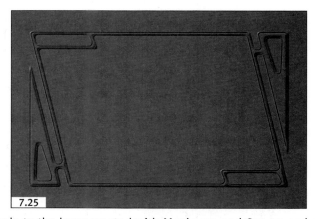

7.25

9. Apply the Darken mode to the layer created with Maximum and Curves and merge the two layers.

10. Load the Template channel and invert the selection. Fill with 128 Red, Green, and Blue by selecting the Eyedropper tool and clicking anywhere in the image with the medium gray color and then press Alt+Delete.

11. Deselect. This will be referred to as the plastic bump map.

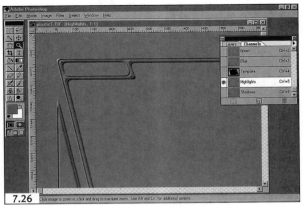

7.26

12. Select all, copy, create a new channel, and paste into the new channel. Name the channel Highlights.

13. Drag the Highlights channel down the New Channel icon (the center icon) in the Channels palette to create a duplicate channel. Name the duplicate channel Shadows.

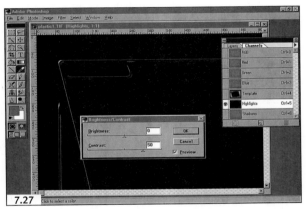

7.27

14. Select the Highlights channel and open Levels (Crtl/Command+L). Click on the black Eyedropper tool and click anywhere in the image on a medium gray spot (the 0 Input Level should change to 128) and then click OK to apply.

15. Use the Brightness/Contrast (Image, Adjust or Ctrl/Command+B) filter to increase the Contrast to approximately 50.

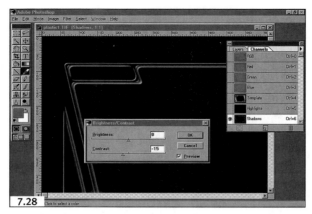

7.28

16. Select the Shadows channel and open Levels. Click on the white Eyedropper tool and click anywhere in the image on a medium gray spot (the 256 Input Level should change to 128), then click OK to apply.

17. Select Invert (Image, Map or Ctrl/Command+I). Use the Brightness/Contrast filter to decrease the Contrast to approximately –15. Delete the plastic bump map layer.

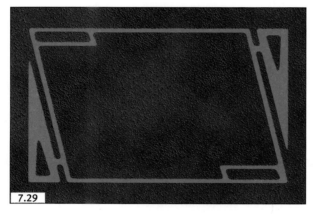

7.29

18. Create an attractive background on the background layer and then create a new layer for the main body of the interface. Select all and delete.

19. Load the Template channel and fill it with a solid color, such as red in this example.

INTERFACE DESIGN with Photoshop

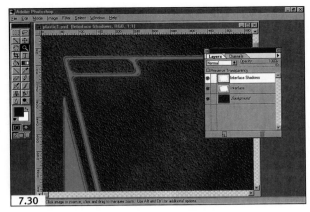

7.30

20. Create a new layer and name it Interface Shadows. Select all and delete.

21. Load the Shadows channel. Click on the foreground color swatch and choose a dark version of whatever color dominates the background or choose a dark color of whatever you want the lightsource to be in. A dark blue was used for this example.

22. Press Alt/Option+Delete to fill the selection with the foreground color and then deselect.

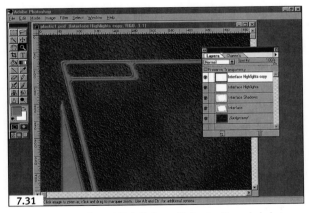

7.31

23. Create a new layer and name it Interface Highlights. Select all and delete.

24. Load the Highlights channel. Click on the foreground color swatch and choose a light version of whatever color dominates the background or choose a light color of whatever you want the lightsource to be in. A light blue was used for this example.

25. Press Alt/Option+Del to fill the selection with the foreground color and then deselect. A duplicate copy of the Highlights layer was created for this example to augment the effect.

7.32

26. Create the buttons with the same technique. The effect shown here is somewhat exaggerated—especially the highlights.

7.33

A green light source.

You can change the color of the light source for an easy variation. For this example, the highlights and shadows were changed to light green and dark green respectively. You can use black and white, but colors can help enhance the appearance of plastic.

7.34

1. To create a Gel effect, start with the basic template on a new layer. As with the plastic effect, the area for the template should be black, and the surrounding areas should be white. Select all, copy, and paste into a new channel named Template.

2. Create a new layer, fill it with white, and name it Gel.

3. Load the Template channel, fill it with black, and deselect.

4. Select the Maximum filter and apply with a radius of 3–5. Apply a Gaussian Blur with a radius that is two more than whatever Maximum value was used. For example, if a Maximum value of 3 was used, apply a Gaussian Blur with a value of 5.

5. Use Curves to apply a curve similar to the one shown in figure 7.24. Try other curves for various effects.

6. Apply Photoshop's Emboss filter with a Height of 2–3 and Amount from 75–150. These steps are similar to those used to create the plastic bump map.

7.35

7. Drag the Gel layer down the new layer icon in the Layers palette to create a duplicate layer (which will automatically be named Gel copy).

8. Select the Move tool and nudge the duplicate Gel layer up and to the left one time. Select the original Gel layer and nudge it down and to the right one time.

9. Select the duplicate layer and apply the Difference layer mode. Merge the two layers. There should be a hairline gray border around the edge of the Gel layer after merging the layers with Difference mode.

10. Change the foreground color to black, Select all (Ctrl/Command + A), and select Stroke from the Edit Menu. Apply a 1 pixel wide stroke.

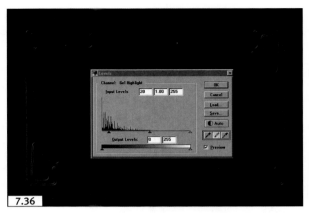

7.36

11. On the Gel layer, Select all and copy. Create two new channels called Gel Highlights and Gel Shadows and paste the contents of the Gel layer into the two new channels.

12. Select the Gel Highlights channel and then select Layers. Replace the Input value of 0 with 20 and select OK to apply.

13. Load the Template channel, invert the selection, and fill with black.

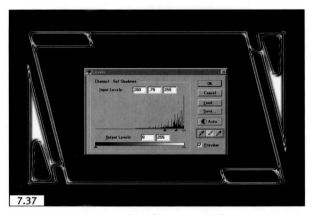

7.37

14. Select the Gel Shadows channel and Invert (Ctrl/Command+I). Select Levels, replace the Input value of 0 to 200 and the 1.00 to .75, and then select OK to apply.

15. Load the Template channel, invert the selection, and fill with black.

INTERFACE DESIGN with Photoshop

7.38

16. Delete the Gel layer.

17. Create two new layers named Gel Highlights and Gel Shadows. Select all on each new layer and delete.

18. Select the Gel Highlights layer, load the Gel Highlights channel, and fill with white.

19. Select the Gel Shadows layer, load the Gel Shadows channel, and fill with black. Adjust the opacity of both layers to 30–50%. Adjust the opacity of the main interface to approximately 70%.

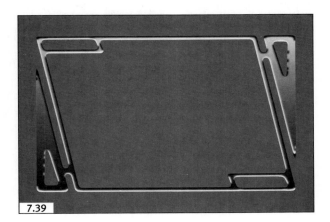

7.39

note

Adobe Gallery Effects' Plaster filter creates an attractive variation for the Gel effect. Create a new layer, name it Gel 2, Select all, and fill with black. Load the Template channel, fill with white, and deselect. Apply a Gaussian Blur with a 3–5 radius. Apply Adobe Gallery Effects' Plaster filter with approximately 25 Image Balance and 7 Smoothness. Load the Template channel, invert the selection, and fill with 128 Red, Green, and Blue (medium gray).

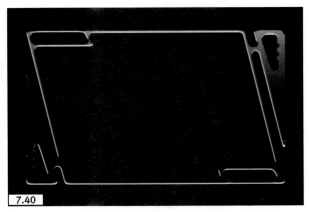

7.40

20. Select all, then copy the Gel 2 layer, create two new channels called Gel 2 Highlights and Gel 2 Shadows, and paste the contents of the Gel 2 layer into the two new channels.

21. Select the Gel 2 Highlights layer and then select Levels. Click on the black Eyedropper tool and click anywhere in the image on a medium gray spot (the 0 Input Level should change to 128) and then select OK to apply.

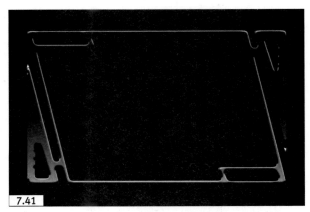

7.41

22. Select the Gel 2 Shadows layer and then select Levels. Click on the white Eyedropper tool and click anywhere in the image on a medium gray spot (the 256 Input Level should change to 128) and then click OK to apply. Select Invert from the Image, Map menu. Delete the Gel 2 layer.

7.42

23. Create two new layers named Gel 2 Highlights and Gel 2 Shadows.

24. Select all on each new layer and delete. Select the Gel 2 Highlights layer, load the Gel 2 Highlights channel, and fill with white.

25. Select the Gel 2 Shadows layer, load the Gel 2 Shadows channel, and fill with black. Adjust the opacity of both layers to 30–50%. Adjust the opacity of the main interface to approximately 70%.

These plastic and gel effects are just a few ways to create a plastic or gel "look." You can also apply the basic emboss effect as shown in Chapter 5, "The Embossed Look," to a solid color to generate a simple plastic look. Plastic looks are also great for the Internet because their simplified color schemes allow them to compress well compared to interfaces with textures.

All the techniques used in this chapter to generate the look of specific materials can be mixed and matched with each other to create other new and interesting effects. See Chapter 9, "Combinations and Unique Variations," for a discussion on creative ways to combine techniques to create unique variations.

CHAPTER 8

The Edge—Random Border Techniques

Straight perfect edges are not always ideal. Random borders provide a sort of dimensional texture that can add to the appeal of an interface. When used with other techniques demonstrated in this book such as the emboss technique and textures, random borders can generate the look of torn paper, holes in walls, and much more. First let's look at the basic approach and then take a look at all the variations.

Covered in this chapter:

► Basic Techniques

► The Tear

► Using Displace

► Other Distort Filters

Basic Techniques

All these techniques begin with the basic shape or template of the button or interface—appearing in black and white within the RGB mode. Most of these techniques work by virtue of the fact that the effect of most filters and effects show up only on the borders of the template, and not within the black area of the template. One little tip before getting started: Creating these edges on separate layers from your original template layer is always a good idea. Coming up with garbage is as easy as coming up with attractive borders. Therefore, make it easy on yourself to go back by experimenting on a copy layer.

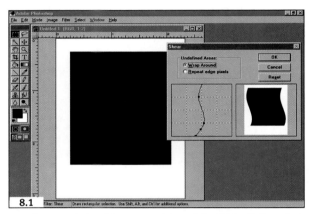

8.1

1. Begin with a basic rectangle template. If you want to add a little flair, rotate the template 90 degrees and apply Shear (Filter, Distort) with a slight S Curve. Rotate the template back to its original position. You can shear the template horizontally instead of vertically without rotating.

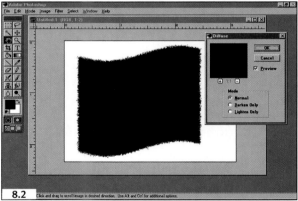

8.2

2. Under Mode, select the Normal option. Apply Diffuse (Filter, Stylize) 10–15 times (press Ctrl/Command+F after the first application to repeat). The effect is cumulative, but the difference between 10 applications and 100 is not very dramatic.

Throughout this chapter, this template will be referred to as the "Rough Template." Adobe Gallery Effects' Spatter is also an excellent source for a similar effect. (Used with express permission. Adobe® and Image Club Graphics™ are trademarks of Adobe Systems Incorporated.)

8.3

The Rough Template is certainly usable as is. The above example, generated with images from PhotoDisc and KPT Power Photos, utilizes the Rough Template to create the interface using techniques from Chapters 3, "Textures from Scratch," 5, "The Embossed Look," and 6, "Shadows, Glows, and Other Bread and Butter Techniques."

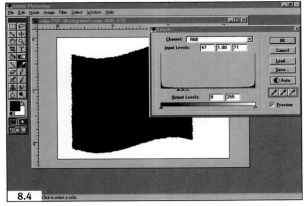

8.4

3. For a less grainy, pixellated edge, apply a slight Gaussian Blur (1–3 radius). Next, collapse the midrange with the Levels dialog box as demonstrated in Chapter 5. Group the Black, White, and Midpoints to the left for a more bumpy result and to the right for a more subtle result.

8.5

4. Softening the edges creates a more subtle effect that calls less attention to itself and looks a little more like torn paper.

This basic effect and its variations represent the fundamental approach to generating random border effects. After generating a border effect on a separate layer or channel using various filter effects, you can use the layer with Layer modes or channel as a selection to create the random border on the interface or interface element.

The Tear

The Tear effect can be used to create a torn paper look that is a little more realistic. Torn paper effects have become somewhat popular as a method of augmenting the sense of a non-computerized environment within the interface.

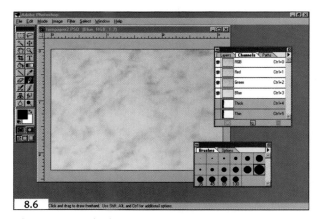

8.6

The torn paper look.

Begin with two or more textures, such as the following from KPT Power Photos, on separate layers. Create a new channel and fill it with white. Select the Pencil tool with a thick brush and draw a random line down or across the page. Use the Paint Bucket tool to fill one side of the line with black. Then, name the channel Thick. Duplicate the channel and choose Filter, Other, Maximum. Use a radius of 4–7 pixels and name this channel Thin. To generate softened edges on each channel, apply a Gaussian Blur and collapse the midrange values as demonstrated for the Rough Template.

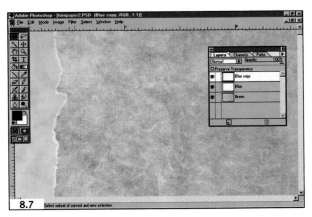

Creating a duplicate layer of the paper texture.

Create a duplicate layer of the texture that will serve as the paper. The duplicate layer should be above the original paper layer. Load the Thick channel on the original paper layer, delete, and deselect. Load the Thin channel on the duplicate paper layer, delete, and deselect. Increase the brightness (Ctrl/Command+B) to 25–35 on the original paper layer.

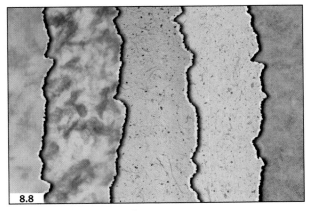

Multiple layers of tear effects.

For multiple layers of tear effects, try to mix up the lines when creating them with the Pencil tool. A nice drop shadow helps the effect substantially (see Chapter 6).

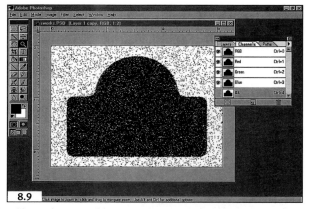

8.9

1. Photoshop's Mezzotint filter also provides some interesting variations. This example began with a template from a vector-based application. The template was blurred with Gaussian Blur, and then Levels collapsed the midtones.

2. The template was copied and pasted into a new channel, and the Maximum filter was applied twice with a radius of 10 each.

3. Then the Pixelate, Mezzotint filter with the Coarse Dots option was applied to the template layer.

8.10

4. Next the Maximum filter was applied with a radius of 1 to spread out the dots. Then a slight Gaussian Blur (2.5) was applied and the midtones were again collapsed with Levels. Notice how this operation has effectively removed the "coarse dots" from around the template.

INTERFACE DESIGN with Photoshop

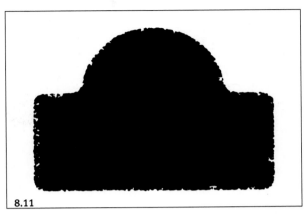

8.11

5. The border looks good, but the holes in the center are not desirable. To remove them, the channel was loaded, inverted, and filled with black. The remaining holes were filled in with the Paintbrush tool by hand. The above example shows this process nearly completed, with only some holes on the left side still remaining.

8.12

6. After all the stray holes were filled in, the results were used in conjunction with the emboss technique demonstrated in Chapter 5 to create an antique sign look using images from PhotoDisc and CMCD.

Using Displace

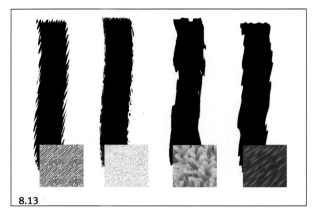

8.13

Borders and edges created from different displacement maps.

Distort, Displace is also an excellent resource for generating creative borders and edges. The examples in figure 8.13 were created from four different displacement maps that come with Photoshop: fragment, mezzo, random, and streaks. The displacement maps can be found in the plug-ins folder within the Photoshop application. Each was applied with approximately 10 horizontal and vertical displacement, Stretch to fit, and Repeat edge pixels.

The trick to using Displace to create border textures is to avoid large values for the displacement. Experiment with displacement between 3–15 horizontally and vertically. Remember that horizontal and vertical displacement do not have to be equal. If a texture creates too much vertical displacement but the horizontal displacement is fine, try it again with less vertical displacement. Increase the contrast within the displacement maps for more grainy borders. Note that random patterns create more haphazard results, whereas regular patterns generate more predictable results.

8.14

Using a texture to create the border effect.

Just about any texture source is valuable for creating displacement maps for border effects. This example was generated with a texture from PhotoDisc that was altered to increase the contrast slightly. Displace was used with 10 horizontal and vertical displacement, Stretch to fit, and Repeat edge pixels.

8.15

Using tiles to generate displacement maps.

You can also create tiles from textures for displacement maps. This example was generated with a texture from PhotoDisc that was altered to increase the contrast slightly and then resized to 200 pixels square. Displace was used with 8 horizontal and vertical displacement, Tile, and Repeat edge pixels. If you look closely, a noticeable pattern exists.

8.16

A more recognizible pattern can be created with different textures.

This example was generated with a seamless tile from Pixar 128 that was resized to 200 pixels square. Displace was used with 8 horizontal and vertical displacement, Tile, and Repeat edge pixels. Notice that the pattern is more recognizable.

Other Distort Filters

Photoshop's other distortion filters provide a wealth of possibilities for attractive borders. These filters include the following:

- ► Ripple
- ► Wave
- ► ZigZag
- ► Polar Coordinates

Ripple

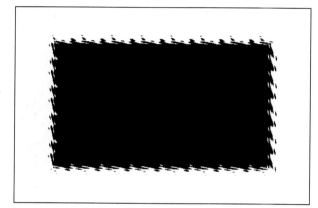

Ripple, Small, Amount: 700.

Ripple, Medium, Amount: 500.

(Used with express permission. Adobe® and Image Club Graphics™ are trademarks of Adobe Systems Incorporated.)

Ripple generates very nice edges. Large Ripples do tend to get out of control quickly whereas Small and Medium Ripples afford more latitude with a wide variety of Amount settings. Adobe Gallery Effects' Ripple filter also generates attractive ripple borders.

Wave

Wave, Type: Sine.

Wave, Type: Square.

Wave generates borders that are obviously indicative of its name. Wave gets out of control quickly. Reign in the wave distortions by reducing the number of generations to one or two and decreasing the scale to 50% or less horizontally and vertically. Decreasing the variation of the Wavelength and Amplitude also helps, creating many possibilities. Try the different types: Sine, Triangle, and Square. Also, utilize the Randomize button to cycle through variations.

ZigZag

ZigZag, Amount: –100, Ridges: 10, Out from Center.

ZigZag, Amount: –20, Ridges: 3, Pond Ripples.

ZigZag generates some really unique borders. Hello Buck Rogers! The Out from Center option generates borders that maintain a consistent horizontal axis more or less, whereas Around Center twists things up. You can always rotate the Around Center distortions back by adjusting the Amount slider. Pond Ripple is a good method to spice up an oval or circular shape. For best results with Pond Ripple, set the Amount slider to the maximum setting, and the Ridges slider at 8–12.

Polar Coordinates

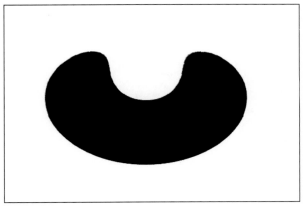

Polar Coordinates, Rectangular to polar on an elliptical source.

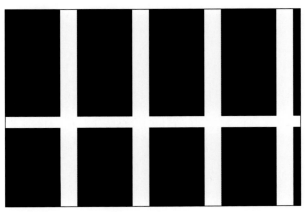

Pattern Source (see Chapter 3).

Polar Coordinates, Polar to rectangular on a rectangle source.

Polar Coordinates, Rectangular to polar on a pattern source.

Finally, Polar Coordinates also can generate some interesting possibilities. Especially interesting results can be generated from such black-and-white patterns as the small rectangular pattern shown above.

All of these techniques can be combined to create even more unusual border effects. For example, try distorting a basic shape with the distortion tools as shown within the "Other Distort Filters" section of this chapter and then apply some of the effects discussed in the "Basic Techniques" section. Organic borders go a long way toward creating an organic feel to interfaces and enable users to forget that they are staring at a flat computer monitor.

CHAPTER 9

Combinations and Unique Variations

Subtle variations on common effects can breathe new life into your interface design. Unique variations can be achieved by experimenting with and mixing the building blocks for the more common effects covered in previous chapters, such as the Highlight and Shadow layers used to build the Emboss effect in Chapter 5, "The Embossed Look." The term "building blocks" is used to refer to the layers that are manipulated in various ways and then used in combination with other layers to generate a final effect.

In this chapter, you review the basic technique for developing combinations, look at methods for building additional building blocks, and finally look at many of the variations possible with the combination technique. Keep in mind that the possibilities are endless, and the following examples serve only as an initial framework for further explorations and variations.

The basic idea behind combinations is to develop a series of layers and channels that can be linked with calculations, layer modes, and opacity. Although it may seem a bit counterintuitive to develop elements with layers that will ultimately be used as channels, generating channels from and with layers often provides much more control and possibilities. The concept of this chapter is to show you how to generate a large number of various building blocks, and then store these in a Photoshop file to be used for generating variations of the final effect. As you become adept at generating variations, try to give the layers descriptive names to help distinguish them. You have up to 32 characters to work with; don't hesitate to use all of them.

Covered in this chapter:

- ► Basic Combination Technique

- ► Embossing and Isolating Highlights and Shadows

- ► Generating "Building Blocks"

- ► Combinations with Layer Modes

- ► Third-Party Filters

Basic Combination Technique

This basic emboss interface covered in Chapter 5 is serviceable, but there are certainly viable alternatives. This example was generated from scratch except for the image from Corel Professional Photos.

Although fig. 9.1 looks fine as it is, there are several combinations that you can apply to make it extraordinary. This figure was developed using the techniques discussed in Chapter 5 using a separate layer for highlights and shadows. The combination technique also relies on using separate layers for highlights and shadows, but it utilizes a different method for developing the highlights and shadows.

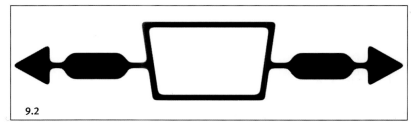

The Main Template.

Begin with a basic template. This template was generated in CorelDRAW!, exported as a Tif, and opened in Photoshop. A small Gaussian Blur was applied and then the black-and-white points were adjusted with the Levels tool to collapse the midtones. We will be building all the variations within one Photoshop file, so drag the Background layer (which should be the "Main Template" at all times) to the new Layer icon in the Layers palette to create a new layer every time you want to generate a new variation.

Create a channel with the Main Template. To do this, select the Main Template layer, Select all, Copy, open the Channels palette, create a new channel, and Paste.

Select Invert (Image, Map) so that the channel selects the interface itself and not its surroundings. Name the new channel Main Template.

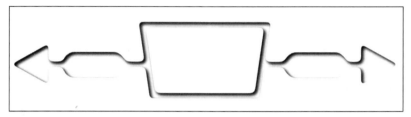

Basic Highlight.

Basic Shadow.

Among the first elements you'll (usually) want to create are the building blocks for basic highlights and shadows.

1. Drag the Background layer or Main Template layer to the New Layer icon in the Layers Palette menu twice to create two new layers.

2. Select the topmost duplicate layer and apply a Gaussian Blur with a 1–3 radius.

3. Select the Move tool, nudge the blurred duplicate down and to the right a few times, and select Invert (Ctrl Command+I) from the Image, Map menu.

4. Select Screen as the layer mode for the blurred duplicate. Merge the blurred duplicate with the other duplicate by turning off all other layers except the two duplicates and selecting Merge Layers from the Layers Palette menu.

5. Rename the new layer Basic Highlights.

6. Repeat this process for a Basic Shadows layer, except nudge the blurred layer up and to the left. This is an alternative approach to the embossed technique demonstrated in Chapter 5.

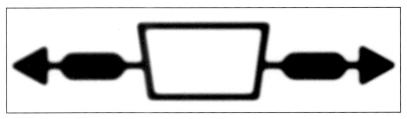

Gaussian Blur.

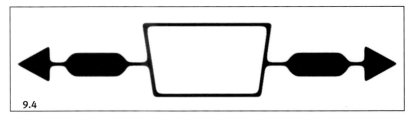

9.4

Maximum/Blur.

It is often useful to generate a few of the basic building blocks that will be used to create additional building blocks to avoid having to repeat the same steps over and over again. Two of the more common are Gaussian Blur and the Maximum effects.

1. Drag the Background layer or Main Template layer to the New Layer icon in the Layers palette twice to create two new layers.

2. Rename the first one Gaussian Blur and apply a Gaussian Blur to it. If you want, you can generate a few layers with various Gaussian Blurs applied and name them appropriately (Gaussian Blur 1 radius, Gaussian Blur 1.5 radius, and so on).

3. Select the other duplicate layer, rename it Maximum/Blur, and apply the Maximum filter and Blur More.

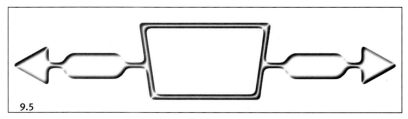

9.5

Difference.

A Difference layer is one of the more valuable building blocks for the combination technique. Its distinctive look is the foundation for many attractive effects.

1. Drag the Background layer or Main Template layer to the New Layer icon in the Layers Palette menu twice to create two new layers.

2. Select the topmost duplicate layer and apply a Gaussian Blur with a 1–3 radius.

3. Select the Move tool and nudge the blurred duplicate down and to the right a few times. Select the other duplicate layer and apply a Gaussian Blur with a 1–3 radius. Select the Move tool and nudge the blurred duplicate up and to the left a few times.

4. Select the topmost layer, select the Difference mode, and merge the two layers. The result will likely have a white border, so fill it with black.

5. Select Invert. Load the Main Template channel. Invert the selection and fill it with white. Invert the selection again.

6. Use Levels to move the black Eyedropper tool's Input levels to 128. You can move the black Eyedropper tool, white Eyedropper tool, and gamma to any position you want for other variations.

7. Deselect and name the layer Difference.

Now that you have a few basic building blocks from which to work, it is time to create some unique effects with the combination technique. Again, this is just the basic technique. We will look at other building blocks and other possibilities with the combination technique later in this chapter.

Embossing and Isolating Highlights and Shadows

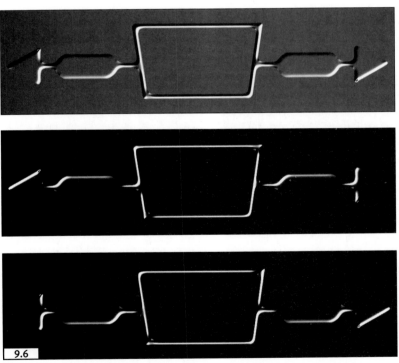

9.6

Unique highlights and shadows can be generated from any number of variations on the Main Template.

This technique can be used to generate an unlimited number of variations. The basic approach is to use Photoshop's Emboss filter on a layer, create a duplicate, and then use Levels to isolate the highlights on one layer and shadows on the other. A channel built from the Main Template layer is used to clip off the effects that are applied beyond the boundaries of the Main Template. This technique is handy for generating unique highlights and shadows from just about any variation. For example, we'll use the Difference layer created in the previous section for the first instance of this approach.

1. Open the Layers Palette menu, create a duplicate of the Difference layer (or whatever layer you want to try this approach on) and apply Emboss (Filter, Stylize). Try various settings; Heights in the 4–5 range and Amounts in the 75–200 range often produce attractive results.

2. Duplicate the embossed layer. Rename the new layers something appropriate, such as Difference Highlight and Difference Shadow for this example.

3. Select the Difference Highlight layer. Load the Main Template channel, use the Eyedropper tool to select a 50% gray, and press Alt+Del to fill the selection with 50% gray. Repeat this process for the Difference Shadows layer. This series of steps will be referred to as "embossing" from here forward.

4. Select the Highlights layer and open the Levels dialog box.

5. Select the white Eyedropper tool in the Levels dialog box, click on a 50% gray pixel anywhere in the image, click OK, and Invert.

6. Select the Shadows layer and open the Levels dialog box. Select the black Eyedropper tool in the Levels dialog box and click on a 50% gray pixel anywhere in the image, then click OK. This series of steps will be referred to as "isolating the highlights and shadows" from here forward.

The results of the emboss variations provide attractive substitutes for Standard Emboss highlights and shadows.

By using these layers as channels to build the highlights and shadows as shown in Chapter 5 under the Calculated Emboss method, the results of the emboss variations provide a unique alternative for the Standard Emboss effect.

After you have an interesting variation, try embossing it to see if you can isolate the highlights and shadows to build yet another unique variation for the interface. Let's look at another quick example, this time using the Gaussian Blur building block you created, to see how easy it is to generate alternatives to the Emboss effect.

INTERFACE DESIGN with Photoshop

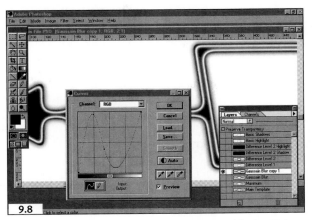

9.8

Apply a curve on the Gaussian Layer copy with the Main Template channel loaded (hidden in this example).

1. Create a duplicate of the Gaussian Blur layer.

2. Use Curves to apply a curve similar to the one shown in figure 9.8. The 75% black Eyedropper tool (lower left segment of the curve) should be moved to somewhere between 235–255 Output, then a point only 10% up the curve should be dragged to about 100 Output, forcing a "U" shape, dip, or valley in the right half of the graph.

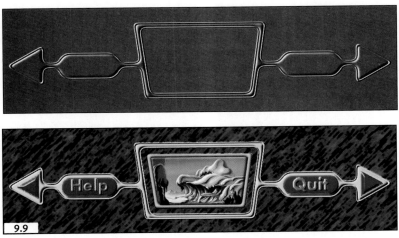

9.9

Another interesting variation is built with the Emboss technique by adding a little curve to a Gaussian Blur.

3. Again, emboss and isolate the highlights and shadows. If you've built the layers in a separate file, cut and paste them as new channels in the file that you are using to generate the actual interface, and use the channels to apply the highlights and shadows as shown in Chapter 5.

To review, the basic idea is to generate some sort of variation of the Main Template, then emboss the results and isolate the highlights and shadows to use them as channels to build highlights and shadows for the real interface. Now let's look at the many other methods that can be used to generate variations. First we will build a few more building blocks, then we will look at more Merge Mode variations. Again, this is not an exhaustive showcase of the possible set of building blocks or the possible variations that can be generated with the Combination technique.

Generating "Building Blocks"

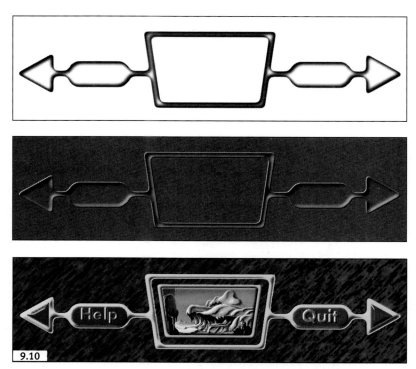

Merge the Highlights and Shadows layers with the Multiply mode.

The more building blocks you have the more possible variations you can generate with the combination technique. The following are a few examples of building blocks that are a good starting point. Use them to create even more building blocks. The idea is to create as many interchangeable building blocks as you can imagine and then experiment with unique combinations.

1. Create duplicates of each of the Basic Highlights and Basic Shadows layers and merge the duplicates with the Multiply mode on the uppermost layer.

2. Rename the merged layer something such as H&S (for Highlights and Shadows). Even this basic effect can lead to an attractive variation.

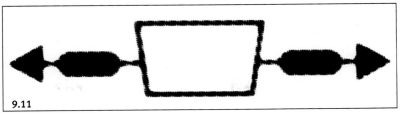

9.11

Ripple Small 250.

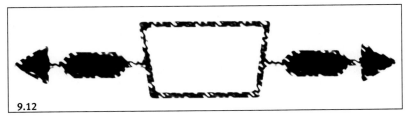

9.12

Ripple Medium 500.

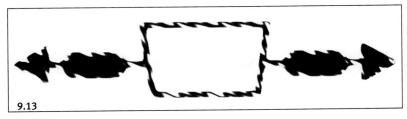

9.13

Ripple Large 200.

1. Create a duplicate of the Gaussian layer.

2. Load the Main Template channel. Invert the selection and fill it with white. Invert the selection again.

3. Select the Ripple filter. The Ripple filter can be used to create a variety of building blocks. Settings from 200–700 with Small, 200–700 with Medium, and 100–200 with Large can all produce interesting results. The idea is to avoid distorting the larger areas—such as the triangular and oval areas in the example—too much. The effects should remain largely on the fringe areas so that the buttons and other objects look like they rest on a reasonable-looking surface.

Try creating several variations using Ripple with different settings. Deselect and name each layer that you create with this Ripple technique with a name that indicates the setting you used, such as Ripple Medium 500.

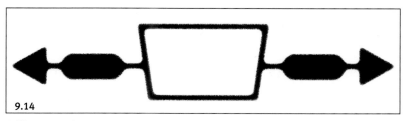

9.14

Diffuse two times.

9.15

Difference Cloud.

9.16

Mezzotint Coarse Dots.

1. Create a duplicate of the Gaussian layer.

2. Load the Main Template channel. Invert the selection and fill it with white. Invert the selection again.

3. Select the Stylize, Diffuse filter two times (using Normal mode). Deselect and name the layer something such as Diffuse. Repeat this process using the Difference Cloud and Mezzotint Coarse Dots (or any of the other Mezzotint variants you prefer) filters.

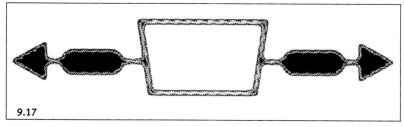

9.17

Curves on the Ripple Small 250 layer.

INTERFACE DESIGN with Photoshop

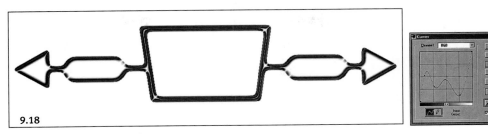

9.18

Curves on the Difference layer.

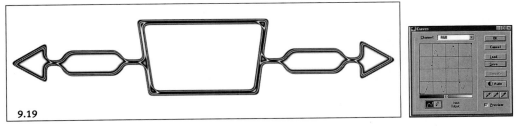

9.19

Curves on the H&S layer (with edge trimmed).

This last series of building blocks utilizes Curves much like the curve technique used in the previous example and those used to generate Chrome effects in Chapter 7, "The Look of Chrome, Glass, and Plastic." Create a duplicate of the building block layers and experiment with various Curve settings. For example, open the Difference layer and open the Curves dialog box. Drag various points along the curve up or down and observe the results with the Preview option selected. Typically, the best results are achieved by creating high areas of contrast within localized tonal ranges. These contrasting areas can be generated by creating a series of high peaks and low valleys along the curve. Name each variant with a name that describes the variant, such as Difference Curves.

> **note**
>
> Often Curve operations on imagery with tight gradients between two colors (black and white in this case) result in jagged edges. To fix this, load the Main Template channel. Select Modify, Contract and contract the selection one pixel. Invert the selection and fill with black. Deselect, load the Main Template channel again, invert the selection, and fill with white. This technique replaces the jagged edges with a consistent color.

Combinations with Layer Modes

9.20

Your Photoshop file after generating all the building blocks.

At this point you should have a Photoshop file with more than a dozen layers that you created through the course of this chapter. The above building blocks are not the only possible variants. Experiment with other filters upon each building block to discover other interesting possibilities. At this point, however, let's look at some of the possible variations created by mixing these building blocks with Layer modes and Opacity settings.

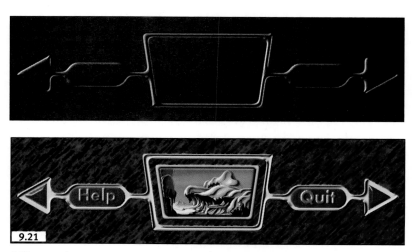

9.21

Difference layer over Gaussian Blur layer with Difference mode.

Using Layer modes substantially increases the possibilities for generating building blocks.

1. Create copies of the Difference and Gaussian Blur layers by dragging them to the New Layer icon in the Layers Palette menu.

2. Position the Difference copy over the Gaussian Blur copy.

3. Select Difference layer and then select Difference from the Mode pop-up menu.

4. Merge the two layers and invert. Emboss and isolate the shadows. The point here is that after you have a few basic template variations, you can merge them with Layer modes and various Opacity settings to create more unique building blocks.

The following examples show the Merge Mode combination and the resulting highlights and shadows on the main sample interface built by embossing and isolating the highlights and shadows. Remember: To combine the building blocks using Layer modes and Opacity settings, create duplicates of the building block layers and combine them by turning off all other layers except the two (or more) that you are working with and selecting Merge Layers from the Layers Palette menu.

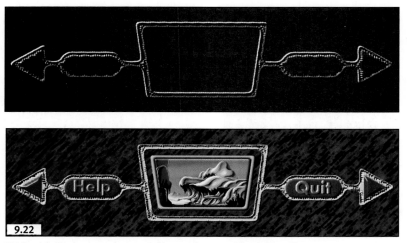

H&S with Darken mode at 100% opacity over Ripple Small 250.

H&S Curves with Darken mode at 80% opacity over Diffuse Difference Clouds with Screen mode at 100% opacity.

Difference with Multiply mode at 100% opacity over Ripple Large 200 with Screen mode at 65% opacity over H&S.

INTERFACE DESIGN with Photoshop

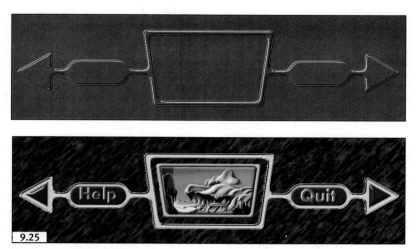

Maximum with Multiply mode at 100% opacity over H&S Curves.

Third-Party Filters

As if all the above techniques were not enough, third-party filters can also provide even more interesting possibilities. In particular, Alien Skin Black Box and Adobe Gallery Effects provide some valuable building blocks that can be used to generate attractive combinations.

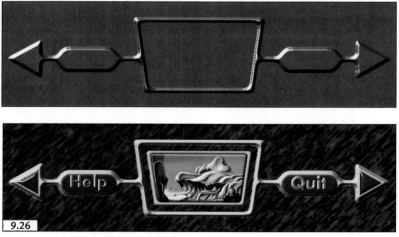

Alien Skin Black Box 2.0 Inner Bevel.

Adobe Gallery Effects' Plaster. (Used with express permission. Adobe® and Image Club Graphics™ are trademarks of Adobe Systems Incorporated.)

Alien Skin's Inner Bevel applied to the H&S Curves Layer.

Alien Skin's Black Box 2.0 Inner Bevel and Adobe Gallery Effects' Plaster also provide useful building blocks. Alien Skin's Inner Bevel can be applied directly to the main image instead of going through the steps of embossing and isolating highlights and shadows. However, going to the trouble of embossing and isolating the highlights and shadows provides more versatility by allowing for additive effects of multiple Highlight and Shadow layers. Inner Bevel works best on a neutral color, so fill a layer with 128 RGB Gray before loading the Main Template channel and applying the filter. Adobe Gallery Effects' Plaster filter works best by inverting a duplicate of the Gaussian Blur layer, loading the Main Template channel, applying Plaster, and then inverting the Main Template channel and filling it with 128 RGB Gray. Interesting variations can also be achieved by applying the third-party filters to duplicates of many of the building block layers.

Again, the techniques demonstrated in this chapter are not comprehensive. Use them as starting points for your own explorations. Whether you are building a simple circle button or a complex multifaceted interface, the techniques described in this chapter can help set your interface elements apart.

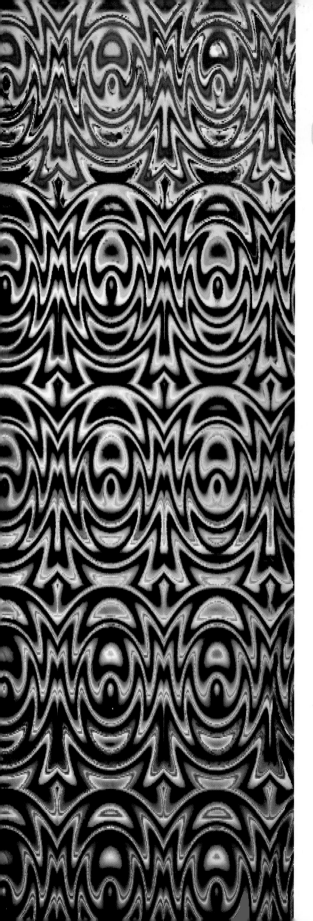

CHAPTER 10

Distortions

Precious little has been written about Photoshop's distortion features. Even though distortion has become the domain of various special effects programs, Photoshop is still a powerful tool capable of generating interesting, valuable, and attractive distortion effects. Distortions are typically used for visual exaggerations: ballooning heads, microscopically thin waists, and so on. Excessive distortions can cause aliasing, so save before attempting distortions so that you can return to a predistorted state if things get out of hand.

Covered in this chapter:

► Using Displace

► Pond Ripple Effect

► Corrugated Pipe

► Walls and Passageways

Using Displace

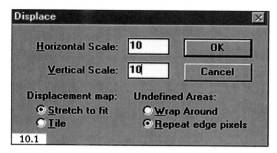

The Displace filter dialog box.

Photoshop's Displace filter is easily its most versatile distortion feature. Displace uses displacement maps to generate its effect. *Displacement maps* are Photoshop files that the Displace filter uses to control its distortion. Because you can build your own displacement maps, the Displace filter provides virtually unlimited possibilities. However, there are certain parameters that you must work within. A complete understanding of how Displace works is necessary to use it effectively.

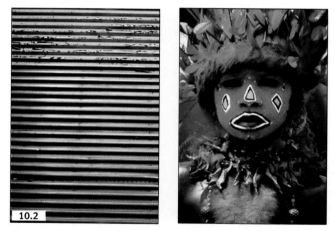

10.2

These images from PhotoDisc and Corel Professional Photos CD-ROM will be used to demonstrate Displace. They are shown here in their predistorted state as a basis of comparison.

Displace employs the color values from a displacement map by using the value to displace an image or selection. A value of 0 (or black) results in the maximum negative displacement (down vertically or to the right horizontally). A value of 255 (or white) results in the maximum positive displacement (up vertically and to the left horizontally). This can be a little confusing because, on an XY graph, positive is up and to the right and negative is down and to the left.

A displacement map with one channel, such as a grayscale file, displaces the image along a diagonal path whose angle is determined by the horizontal and vertical scale ratios. A displacement map with more than one channel, such as a grayscale file with an alpha channel, displaces the image horizontally according to the first channel, and vertically according to the second. A displacement map can be any Adobe Photoshop file except a bitmap.

If the displacement map is not exactly the same size as the image, you have two options at your disposal: Stretch to Fit or Tile. Stretch to Fit can produce chunky results if the map is a lot smaller than the image, and Tile often produces undesirable results except when the map is a seamless tile. The Displace filter moves pixels off the screen or pushes them from the edges. Displace enables you to choose between Wrap Around and Repeat Edge Pixels to deal with this.

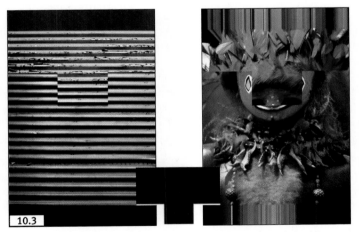

10.3

A single channel displacement map was used to distort the original image.

Figure 10.3 was altered with a single-channel grayscale displacement map. The map was created with the same dimensions as the sample files (refer to fig. 10.2). The Displace options entered in the Displace Filter dialog box were Horizontal 0 and Vertical 50, and the Repeat Edge Pixels option was used to show the effect a little more clearly. When a map and an image have the same dimensions, Stretch to Fit and Tile produce the same results, so it does not matter which option you use.

Observe the results. The black portion of the map displaced the top part of the image down the maximum negative value (down Vertical 50) and the white portion of the map displaced the bottom part of the image up the maximum positive value (up Vertical 50). Notice that the distortion has hard edges due to the lack of grayscale in the displacement map.

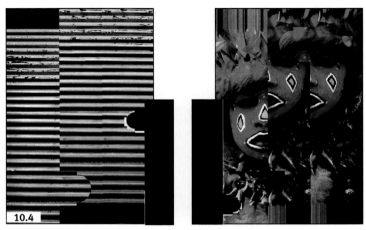

A single channel displacement map was used to distort the original image.

1. These images were altered with a dual-channel grayscale displacement map (shown above between the two sample images, channel 1 on the left and channel 2 on the right).

2. Set the Displace options to Horizontal 50 and Vertical 50, with the Repeat Edge option active.

3. Create the dual-channel grayscale displacement map by pasting a copy of the file into a new channel and then horizontally and vertically flipping the selection.

The results are a little trickier to interpret visually. Channel 2 from the displacement map displaced the image vertically, the black portion pushing the image down 50 pixels (visible on the right side of each example) and the white portion pushing the image up 50 pixels (visible on the left side of each example). Channel 1 from the displacement map displaced the image horizontally, the black portion pushing the image to the right 50 pixels (not visible in either example) and the white portion pushing the image to the left 50 pixels (visible in the center of each example). This demonstrates that a hierarchy exists: vertical over horizontal, left over right. Thus, some parts of the distortion will overlap others, making the results somewhat unpredictable.

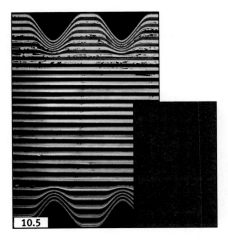

10.5

1. These images were altered with a dual-channel grayscale displacement map (shown above between the two sample images not to scale, channel 1 on the left and channel 2 on the right).

2. Set the Displace options to Horizontal 0 and Vertical 75, with the Repeat Edge option active.

3. Create the dual-channel grayscale displacement map by filling the main file with RGB values of 128 each (Red 128, Green 128, and Blue 128).

4. Create the bumps in the alpha channel (channel 2) in a vector-based application, import into Photoshop, and then Gaussian Blur. The bumps both blur into RBG values of 128 each.

The results are much more useful than the first two examples. Channel 2 from the displacement map displaced the image vertically, the black portion pushing the image down 75 pixels and the white portion pushing the image up 75 pixels. By blending the black and white into the 128 gray, the distortion is given a gradual transition. Channel 1 from the displacement map does nothing because it is entirely 128 gray. Because the first channel in a dual-channel map controls horizontal distortion and the second controls vertical distortion, this map was built to only vertically distort the image by giving the horizontal displacement function nothing to work with.

> **note**
>
> Incidentally, Displace works the same if the displacement map used for figure 10.5 is in a single-channel diplacement map. When there is no transition from the plus and minus level 128, a single-channel map works similarly to a dual-channel map.

It would be relatively easy to make a selection and delete the repeated pixels left from the Displace filter's Repeat edge pixels option in the left image. Its edge pixels happen to be fairly uniform in color. The image on the right, however, would be a little more difficult to select and remove the repeated pixels.

10.6

Adding a color border using Displace.

One strategy for dealing with the problem of removing the results of the Repeat edge pixels option is to increase the canvas size a pixel or two all the way around the image with black, white, or any other easily selected color as the background color. This keeps the main image intact while adding a uniform color border. When you apply the Displace filter with the Repeat edge pixels option selected, the repeated color is uniform and thus easier to select. You can resize the canvas to its original size after applying the Displace filter. The size of the file will be bigger if you increase the canvas size, so you should make your displacement map fit the expanded size or you should use the Stretch to fit option.

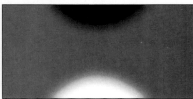

10.7

Distorting an image of a two dollar bill to create a unique visual effect.

Here's an example of how you might use the Displace filter to perform a special effect. This example was created with images from CMCD and PhotoDisc. The displacement map was created in a vector-based application at the approximate cropped size of the two dollar bill, imported into Photoshop, Gaussian Blurred, and then saved as a single-channel grayscale Photoshop file. The canvas of the two dollar bill was then slightly increased with black as the background. After the Displace filter was applied with a Vertical setting of 50, the image was cut and pasted as a layer into the file with the clamp and background.

Note that the gradual blend from white to medium gray and from black to medium gray causes the effect to be applied smoothly. The medium gray tones from the displacement map result in no displacement. This is the key to building displacement maps for controlled distortions. By blending the white and black tones in a displacement map into medium gray tones, you can selectively apply distortions to an image.

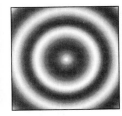

Creating a unique texture using the Displace filter.

The Displace filter also can be the tool of choice to create an unlimited variety of visual effects. This effect was generated from the image shown in figure 10.2, using Displace with the Tile and Wrap Around options. If you're trying to create wild textures with Displace using tiles, try using displacement maps that have contrasting shapes to the main image. See Chapter 8, "The Edge—Random Border Techniques," for a discussion about using the Displace filter to generate random edges.

Here are a few other tips for creating displacement maps:

► When building displacement maps, use Levels to replace black values with 128 gray—replacing 0 with 128 in the output setting within the Levels dialog box. This converts the shadows to medium gray as needed.

► When building displacement maps, use Levels to replace white values with 128 gray—replacing 255 with 128 in the output setting within the Levels dialog box. This converts the highlights to medium gray as needed.

► The High Pass Threshold filters in conjunction with Gaussian Blur and the preceding suggestions can be valuable for creating random displacement maps.

Pond Ripple Effect

Many other distortion filter effects can be used to create interesting and attractive effects. This brief tutorial demonstrates how to create a pond ripple effect with the Polar Coordinates and ZigZag filters. Although a pond ripple effect isn't the most called-upon effect in interface design, its effect is visually appealing and can be used liberally on buttons and animations for a liquid-oriented theme, for example. Besides, you know what they say about all work and no play.

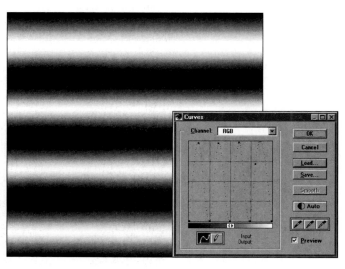

Adding various elements to complete the interface.

1. A visual effect of water rippling can be generated with a series of distortion filters. This effect works slightly better at lower resolutions, so if you're trying it at 72 ppi, it may look somewhat different than shown here. Begin with a black to white linear gradient. Use the Image, Adjust, Curves option to create the wild gyrations shown in the example.

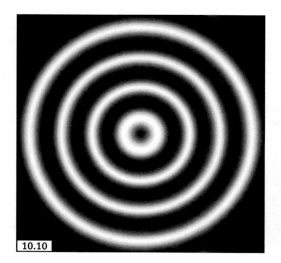
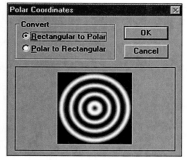

2. To create gradient rings, use Polar Coordinates (Filter, Distort) with the Rectangular to Polar option selected. Note that the slight streaks extending from the outermost ring in the preceding example are more common to high-resolution distortions with the Polar Coordinates filter.

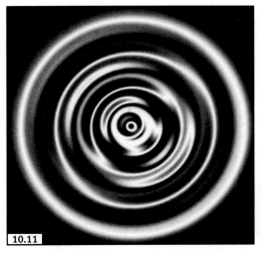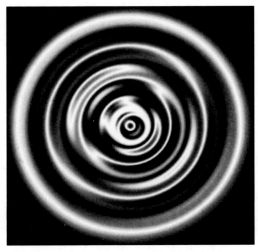

10.11

Amount −25.   *Amount 25.*

3. Now select the ZigZag filter (Filter, Distort), choose the Pond ripples option, and set Ridges to 5–7. The appropriate Amount setting depends on the resolution of the file. For low resolution files, use small amounts between plus or minus 10. Settings of plus or minus 35 are more appropriate for high-resolution files.

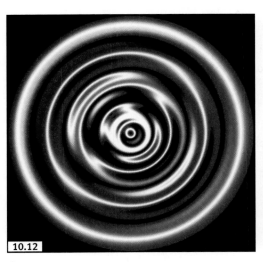

10.12

Amount −25.   *Amount 25.*

4. After you have the ripple effect you can colorize with Hue/Saturation or distort it further with the Image, Effects features such as the distortion above created with Perspective. The pond ripple effect can also be used to create a little GIF animation because the effect of the ripple going from its positive and negative extremes creates a smooth transition.

> **note**
>
> The image (or portion of the image) that you are going to manipulate must be on a separate layer for any of the Image, Effects features to work.

Corrugated Pipe

This short tutorial demonstrates the Shear filter. Shear distorts horizontally. If you need to Shear vertically, rotate the image 90 degrees. Like pond ripple, corrugated pipe isn't necessarily a commonly used interface design element, but Shear's effect is a valuable distortion tool that interface designers should be familiar with.

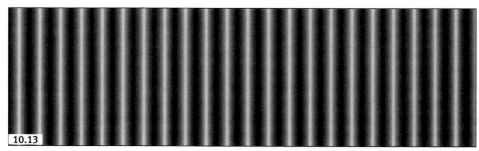

10.13

1. Begin with a short wide file (for instance, this example was created from an approximately 3 inch wide by 1 inch tall file) filled with a corrugated fill, created with the Pattern Fill feature, as shown in Chapter 3, "Textures from Scratch." Use Highlights that are not completely white and shadows that are not completely black.

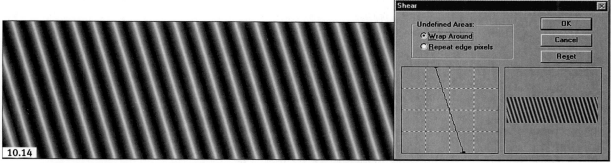

10.14

2. Use Shear (Filter, Distort) with the Wrap Around option activated to angle the corrugated fill. Shear's Wrap Around feature leaves some artifacts where it wraps. These can easily be cleaned up by selecting the artifacts with the Lasso selection tool and then applying Blur or Blur More a few times.

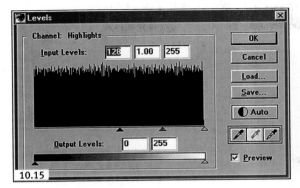

10.15

3. Open the Channels palette, create a new channel by clicking on the New Channel icon in the bottom center, and name it Highlights. Fill the Highlights channel with a linear Gradient Fill from black to white, black on the bottom and white on the top. Use Levels to adjust the Input black point to 128, forcing black up from the bottom to the vertical center of the channel. Drag the Highlights channel to the new channel icon and rename the duplicate Shadows. Select All (Ctrl/Command+A), select Image, Flip, Vertical, and deselect (Ctrl/Command+D).

10.16

4. Load the Highlights channel and apply the Brightness/Contrast (Ctrl/Command+B) filter with brightness set to 100 and contrast set to –90 to create the highlights. Deselect (Ctrl/Command+D) the Highlights channel, load the Shadows channel, and use the Brightness/Contrast filter with –100 and –90 respectively to create the shadows. Return to the composite RGB channel (Ctrl/Command+O).

Walls and Passageways

Distortions can also be made with Photoshop's Image, Effects filters. These effects generate straightforward distortions. Photoshop's Image, Effects filters are particularly handy for generating quick passageways that are common to many of the virtual worlds in multimedia. 3D programs do a better job rendering dimensional passageways, but Photoshop can do a passable job, especially with strategic placement of shadows.

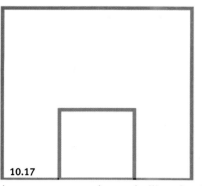

10.17

1. You can render passageways by eyeballing the distortions, but I prefer to use a template from a vector-based application. Begin with any texture, such as this one from Screen Caffeine Pro.

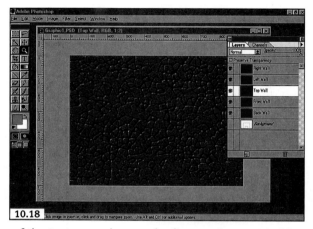

10.18

2. Create four duplicates of the texture and name the five versions something such as the following: Front Wall, Back Wall, Right Wall, Left Wall, and Top Wall. Position the Front and Back Wall below the rest of the layers.

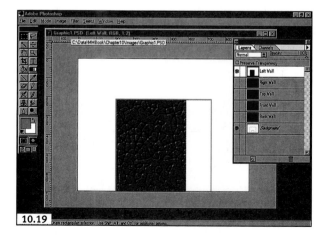

10.19

3. Turn off all the layers except the Left Wall layer and the Template layer. Be sure the Left Wall layer is active and start by deleting excess texture, using the template as a guide. The idea is to remove a lot of texture so the texture doesn't become completely unrecognizable when it's distorted.

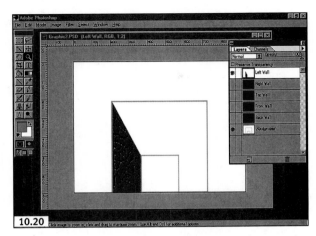

10.20

4. Use Image, Effects Distort to position the Left Wall layer, using the template as a guide. The Distort feature enables the movement of each corner independently. Using Distort, however, means that it takes slightly longer for the preview to redraw. Click anywhere inside the selection to apply the distortion and anywhere outside to cancel and start over. Usually you can overcompensate with the distortion. Wait for the screen to redraw, then position the distortion correctly, using the template as a guide.

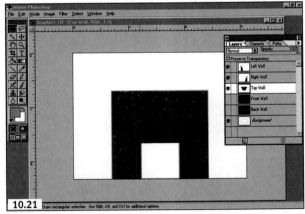

10.21

5. Repeat the process for the Right and Top Wall layers. Leaving the completed layers on as guides can also help.

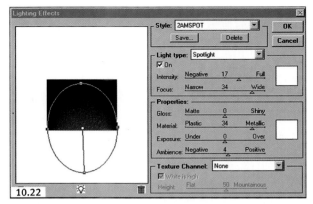

10.22

6. Use Image, Effects, Scale to resize the Back Wall layer to about a quarter of its original size. Select the Move tool and reposition the Back Wall layer behind it in the center of the Right, Left, and Top Wall layers. Use Lighting Effects (Filter, Render) to add lighting to the Back Wall layer. This example was created with a downward spotlight that helped generate a slightly curved shadow.

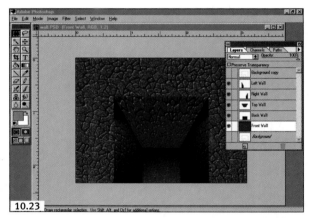

10.23

7. Make sure that the Front Wall layer is below all of the other layers (except the template). Use Curves or Brightness/Contrast to lighten up the Front Wall Layer. Apply Lighting Effects to the Right and Left Wall layers. Angled spotlights were used for this example.

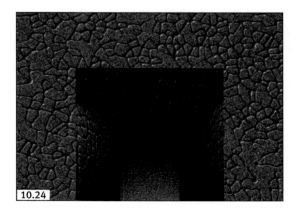

10.24

8. Use Brightness/Contrast to darken the Top Wall layer. Try to leave a little detail. Turn on all of the layers and merge.

Using a third-party program to distort features and images.

Specialized distortion software programs, such as Metatool's Goo and Elastic Reality Inc.'s Elastic Reality, are also available to generate more complex distortions. Metatool's Goo is notable in that it is easy to use and works best with low-resolution images. Beyond its capabilities, Metatool's Goo is another example of excellent interface design. Notable features include controls that fade in and out when the cursor rolls over and off of them. Special effects programs like Elastic Reality apply distortions less interactively. Users are required to define the shapes of the distortions using Bézier lines and shapes similar to those found in most popular vector-based applications.

Although distortions are not commonly needed for daily interface design requirements, it pays to develop skills with Photoshop's distortion tools. Subtle distortions on interface design elements, such as buttons and video screens, help give a more organic feel to interfaces and more pronounced special effect-oriented distortions help augment the visual interest of the imagery within an interface as well as on the imagery the interface is featuring. Avoid excessive distortions that will detract from the intuitiveness of the interface or overly disturb the user. When you've mastered Photoshop's distortion tools, you will be able to integrate distortions ranging from mild to wild into your interfaces.

CHAPTER 11

Vector and 3D Imagery

Adobe Photoshop is not ideally suited for generating some types of imagery. Vector-based applications such as Adobe Illustrator, CorelDRAW!, and Macromedia FreeHand are more capable of creating and manipulating basic shapes. Three-dimensional applications such as Ray Dream Studio, Macromedia Extreme 3D, and Auto·Des·Sys formz Renderzone are more capable of generating 3D imagery. Nevertheless, Photoshop is often used to augment imagery from these types of applications and to prepare imagery for use with applications such as bump maps and texture maps.

Covered in this chapter:

► Using Photoshop with Vector-Based Applications/Templates

► Using Photoshop with 3D Applications

Using Photoshop with Vector-Based Applications/Templates

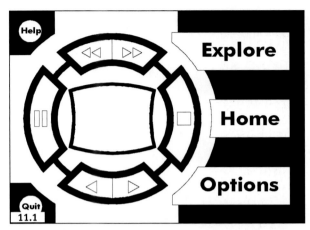

This template, used to generate one of the interfaces in Chapter 7, was created in CorelDRAW!.

Vector-based applications are often used in interface design to generate templates. Vector-based applications are more adept at creating shapes and performing general layout tasks such as aligning and setting text. Although this book is about Photoshop, we will take a look at which kinds of operations are best performed in a vector-based application for interface design, and then imported into Photoshop for the finishing touches. These operations include the following:

► Creating basic and complex shapes

► Creating and aligning text

► Creating precise layouts

► Creating easy to edit templates

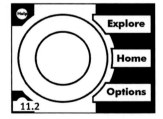 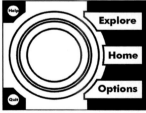 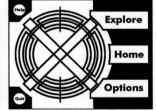 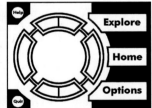

Shapes that are difficult to create in Photoshop are easy for a vector-based application.

Although this is a Photoshop book, it is valuable to look at complex shape creation in a vector-based application. Some tasks are best left to programs other than Photoshop. To create the circular element of the interface, a large circle was drawn. A feature called Contour was used to create an inset version of the original circle about .365 inches inside the original. The Contour feature was then used to create two other circles .155 inches inside the original outer circle and outside the inner circle. The outermost and innermost circles were combined, and a rotated circle was used to trim the diagonal stripe from their combined shape. Contour was used again on the resulting shapes to create the buttons. A line was drawn over the top and bottom buttons to cut them in half with Trim. Finally, the two inner circles were combined and welded to the shapes created with rotated rectangles.

Most major vector-based applications have features that enable welding and trimming shapes to and from each other as well as contouring features that enable shapes to be expanded or contracted. In addition, most vector-based applications have alignment, positioning, and sizing features that provide for complete precision of shape creation and placement. Text is much easier to edit and position in vector-based applications.

Templates created in vector-based applications should be created and exported at the exact size and resolution that they will be used within Photoshop. To export templates at the exact size and be sure that the elements will all be positioned correctly, create a white background the exact dimensions of the interface. A 640×480 interface is 8.889 inches wide by 6.667 inches high. All elements can be created relative to this white background so that they will be positioned correctly. If necessary, each element in the vector-based application can then be exported separately with the white background to ensure each piece will be in the correct position.

The Collapsing Midtones Technique

One of the more common techniques referred to in this book for preparing vector-based templates within Photoshop is using Levels to "collapse the midtones" of a template that has had Gaussian Blur applied to it. Although this technique is discussed in other parts of the book, let's take a close look at this technique now to better understand its value and limitations.

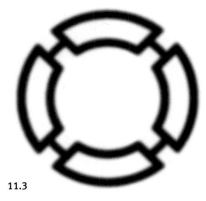

11.3

Adding various elements to complete the interface.

1. Figure 11.3 shows a template with Gaussian Blur with a radius of 6 applied to it (keep in mind that these images were created at 300 ppi for this book; a radius of 6 might be too high for 72 ppi multi-media purposes).

   The amount of Gaussian Blur that is applied to a template must stay within certain constraints and depends on the desired effect. Too much Gaussian Blur will make the template an undefined blob. With Gaussian Blur, pixels are blurred inside and outside from the point of origin of an outline. This Gaussian Blur blurred the template 3 pixels inside and outside the outlines of the shape. If a radius of 20 were used, the shape would be almost unrecognizable.

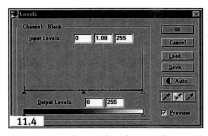 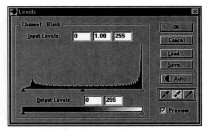

11.4

2. The screen capture on the right shows the template's histogram before Gaussian Blur was applied. Notice that the greatest concentrations are in the black-and-white spectrums of the histogram with a tiny bit of registration in the midtones due to anti-aliasing. The screen capture on the left shows the template's histogram after Gaussian Blur was applied. Notice that there is now a small concentration of dark tones on the right with a fairly even distribution of midtones created by the Gaussian Blur filter between the concentration of white tones on the left.

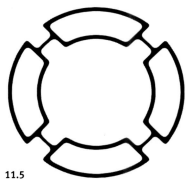 

11.5

3. In this example, the Levels feature was used to collapse the midtones to the left. The black-and-white input values were changed to 40 and 70 from 0 and 256 respectively. Note that the template is now fairly skinny. This demonstrates that when the midtones are collapsed to the left, the resulting template is skinnier.

11.6

4. For this example, the Levels feature was used to collapse the midtones to the right. The black-and-white input values were changed to 160 and 190 from 0 and 256 respectively. Note that the template is now fairly fat. This demonstrates that when the midtones are collapsed to the right, the resulting template is fatter.

Collapsing the midtones too much causes aliasing along the edges of the template. A general rule of thumb is to keep a distance of approximately 30 levels between the black-and-white points. Notice that collapsing the midtones causes subtle curves to be generated within the sharp corners of the interface. This helps make the interface look less mechanical and more fluid. See Chapter 13 "Sliders, Dials, Switches, Doodads, and Widgets" for more examples of using vector-based applications with Photoshop.

Using Photoshop with 3D Applications

Three-dimensional applications are often used in interface design to generate complex 3D imagery. Although Photoshop is capable of some 3D effects, it cannot match the modeling and rendering capabilities of most entry-level 3D applications. Photoshop often plays an integral role in generating 3D imagery for interface design, however, both by providing bump maps and texture maps that the 3D applications can use and with post-production of 3D images and animations.

Three-dimensional applications such as Ray Dream Designer use bump maps to apply bump surface effects. Bump maps enable 3D applications to generate 3D surfaces that would otherwise be extremely difficult to model within the 3D application. Grayscale images are used (color images are typically converted to grayscale) to control the effect. White areas generate the high areas and black areas generate the low areas. 50% gray tones translate into flat areas. The 3D models are not actually warped using the bump maps. Instead, the lighting applied to the 3D model is affected so that the perception of a bump map is created, much like the standard emboss effect. Photoshop's Gaussian Blur filter is valuable for creating bump maps because gradients enable a smooth transition from the high and low points of a bump surface.

Texture maps are bitmapped textures that 3D applications use to wrap onto models. Texture maps either need to be seamless or larger than the 3D models that they will be wrapped on; otherwise, unsightly seams might appear. Texture maps can be created from any image or texture created with or exported from Photoshop.

Tony Jones, with Sun Dog Limited, used Photoshop throughout the process of creating his interactive CD-ROM for his portfolio. Although the majority of the imagery was created with Ray Dream Studio, Photoshop played an integral role in preparing the 3D images by providing bump maps and texture maps, adjusting the 3D images after they were rendered, and preparing them for use with Macromedia Director.

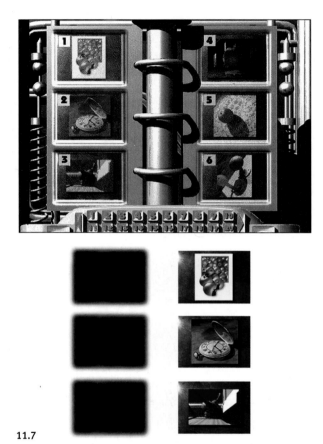

11.7

1. After modeling the main interface in Ray Dream Studio, Tony opened Photoshop and created a file with the same dimensions and resolution as the interface in Ray Dream Studio. He then drew a series of rectangles and applied Gaussian Blur to them. Tony saved the file in TIFF and loaded the blurred rectangles as bump maps within Ray Dream Studio to create the recessed frames for the images.

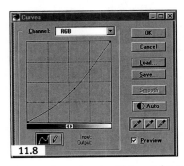

11.8

2. Next, Tony needed to adjust the color and contrast of his 3D images. Renderings from 3D applications tend to need adjustments with Photoshop. It is typically easier to adjust contrast and color in Photoshop than to attempt to rerender the 3D image. Tony wanted this interface to have more contrast and be richer, so he used Photoshop's curves to increase the shadows while decreasing the highlights. Before applying the curve, he saved the curve so that he could load it and apply it to other renderings from Ray Dream for his interactive CD-ROM. After adjusting the curves as previously shown, Tony used Photoshop's retouching tools to clean up artifacts and flaws in the interface left over from the rendering process.

11.9

3. Tony had to turn to Photoshop to generate the button up and down states for the interface. To do this, Tony rendered three different versions of the interface from Ray Dream Studio: one version with the buttons in their up state, one version with the buttons in their down state, and one version without any buttons. Tony then used Photoshop to mask and save separate copies of each button in each state. After the buttons were saved, Tony imported the up state buttons into Macromedia as cast members and then used Lingo to access the down state copies when the buttons were clicked.

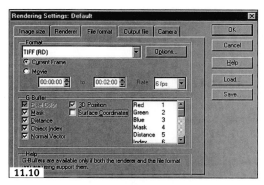

Ray Dream Studio's G-Buffer options.

In addition to using bump maps from Photoshop to create the buttons and casing for this variation, Tony also applied the curve and built the button up and down states in the same way as in the preceding example. To create the depth of field effect on the picture of the apples, Tony used the distance mask that Ray Dream Studio creates. A distance mask uses the distance each model is from the camera when the image is rendering within a 3D application to generate a mask. The farther away the 3D element is, the less the mask. Tony used this mask to apply a Gaussian Blur so that the 3D apples that were farthest from the front received the most blurring. Many 3D applications such as Ray Dream Designer provide options for creating various selections that are generated with the 3D rendering. These selections are loaded as channels in Photoshop and can be used to create special effects and edits on the 3D image.

By using Photoshop with other applications that perform specialized tasks, interface designers can generate just about any kind of image or virtual world they can imagine. Although some of the tasks that can be performed in vector-based applications and 3D applications can be done more laboriously in Photoshop, using the right tool for the job saves money, time, and energy. Photoshop, despite its limitations in generating images, was not designed to create; nevertheless, it is an integral part of the vast majority of interface design projects.

INTERFACE DESIGN with Photoshop

CHAPTER 12

Working with Stock Images in Interface Design

Not everything you use in your interface can be generated efficiently from scratch from within Photoshop. Using stock imagery, scans, and other source imagery such as screen captures and video stills is often required to meet deadlines or acquire just the right element for a project. Most images require a little dressing up or alteration to fit into the character of the project. You will often want to do one or both of the following two things with an image: either display it as crisply and attractively as possible, or apply some sort of visual effect to it. This chapter takes a brief look at image correction techniques and masking techniques, and then rounds things off with several fun and useful visual effects that can help a stock image not *look* like a stock image.

Covered in this chapter:

- ► Why Stock Images?

- ► Correcting the Images

- ► Button Up and Down States

- ► Collage and the Non-Static Interface

- ► Special Effects

- ► Other Interesting Possibilities

Why Stock Images?

Although a skilled designer can render just about anything he might need with Photoshop, it is typically easier to alter an existing image. With Photoshop, it is relatively easy to make an image from a stock photography collection look like it naturally fits into the interface as opposed to rendering something from scratch. Unless you happen to be a well-traveled photographer, you probably don't have all of the types of images you may need on hand to integrate into your interface. Stock photography collections are often the answer because they strive to both provide a wide variety of subjects and also to fill specialized needs.

For example, say you have a interface with a tropical theme. Instead of rendering palm leaves, coconuts, and a tribal mask from scratch, it would be much easier to acquire these from stock images. Stock photography collections typically include images for most popular themes. Many vendors, such as Corel Corporation, sell hundreds of collections with specialized subjects. These images can easily be cut and pasted into the interface file and then integrated using Photoshop's retouching tools, color correction features, and filters. At the very least, they can serve as a template for an image rendered from scratch in Photoshop.

With the phenomenon of CD-based stock photography collections and stock images being sold via the web, it is easy to economically acquire virtually any image that might be needed. If you happen to have an image that you can scan or have scanned, that's even better. Other ways of economically acquiring images include video captures, digital cameras, and screen captures.

Stock images are limited to the scope of their licensing agreements; however, this is usually not a major problem. Typically, stock images can be used within multimedia and web titles as long as they are not being sold on them. In other words, if you are selling another vendor's stock image on your multimedia title or web site, you can expect a certified letter notifying you of your court date. Most images on the web can easily be acquired either by screen capture or by downloading the image. The web contains a vast supply of uncopyrighted images, but copyrighted images on the web are off limits. Always check the licensing agreement of your stock photography vendor before shipping your title. Even though stock images can easily be altered beyond recognition, a lawsuit is a good way to ruin the financial success of any multimedia venture.

Correcting the Images

Most images can and should be augmented for use with multimedia and the web. Even color corrected stock images are often too gray or have a bit of a color cast to them. Furthermore, many images need to be adjusted to fit within the context of the multimedia title. You might adjust an image to conform to a particular color group that dominates an interface or adjust an image to increase its contrast with the surrounding interface to make it stand out more.

Unlike images that are being prepared for print media, you can largely use how the image looks on your monitor as a meter for how it will look in the final product. You should always test your images on the target screen size and color depth. If you have reason to believe that your market will only be viewing your multimedia title or web page on a 640×480 screen with 256 colors, then you should optimize the image for that market. Usually the best way to prepare for curve manipulations is to start with the Levels tool.

Levels

Some of the more fun features in Photoshop—such as plug-in filters and layers—have been widely discussed, but relatively little has been written about two of Photoshop's more powerful bread and butter features: Levels and Curves. The Levels and Curves features are a little more technically oriented than many of the other features in Photoshop, but after they are fully understood, Levels and Curves can be extremely valuable tools for photo touchup and special effects.

It may be easy to see that an image looks murky or otherwise out of balance, but it can be much more difficult to figure out how to correct the problem. The problem is compounded when you are dealing with a color image, such as CMYK or RGB, because of the additional channels you must deal with. Often the answer to this problem begins with the Levels tool and with learning how to read a histogram.

This image looks fine as it is, but it can be improved.

This image has been cropped from a Corel Professional Photos' CD-ROM collection. To the untrained eye this image may look fine and, indeed, it may be exactly how the artist originally wanted it to look. This example image has too much tonal concentration in the lower or darker midrange, however, and can be made to look crisper with a small adjustment.

Repositioning the black-and-white points increases the contrast in most images by giving the images some true blacks and true whites and by spreading out the midtones so that they are not so bunched up in one area. You should adjust the Levels of almost any image in preparation for curve manipulation. By remapping the black-and-white points with the Levels tool, you can give the Curves tool a more tonally balanced image with which to work.

Reading Histograms

To use the Levels tool you will need to know a little about histograms. The histogram of an image can be viewed by selecting Histogram from the Image menu. Histograms provide a digital picture of an image. The information in a histogram provides insights as to how an image can be optimized. A histogram maps the distribution of tones in an image in a selected channel or the brightness levels with the Gray channel. It plots the number of pixels at each brightness or tonal level. The horizontal axis maps the color values from darkest (0) at the far left to brightest (255) at the far right. The handy gradient under the histogram makes it easy to interpret this axis. The higher a line on a histogram, the more pixels the brightness or tonal level has in the image. A histogram for a dark image would have most of its pixels at the left side of the graph. A histogram for a light image would be more heavily weighted to the right side.

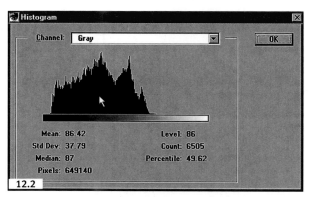

A histogram maps the distribution of tones.

With the histogram it is easy to see a large concentration of pixels in the approximately 50%–90% black tonal range (between levels 20 and 140), which partially explains the murkiness of the image. Notice, also, that no pixels are completely white or completely black. In fact, no pixels have tones of approximately 40% white or lighter and 95% black or darker. In general, it is better for an image's histogram to be more evenly distributed (this is less true for artwork than it is for images from the real world, but it's still a fairly accurate rule of thumb). In addition, the contrast in most images will benefit greatly from having pixels that have 100% and 0% tones of a given ink (black in a grayscale image). This is not a hard rule, however, because some images don't lend themselves to even tonal distribution. An image of a black crow perched in front of a white barn, for instance, likely wouldn't afford much room for tonal distribution.

Notice that the median is 87. The median is the middle value in the range of brightness or color values in the image. It is the brightness or tonal halfway point. Drag the mouse over the histogram and notice that the Levels readout changes as you drag left to right. The far left is 0 (black) and the far right is 255 (white). If the image were balanced, it would have a median closer to 128 (half of 256, the total number of tonal values). Thus, this image has a Median value that is on the dark side. Again, for some images this may be absolutely perfect, but often an image will benefit from an attempt to bring this value closer to the center.

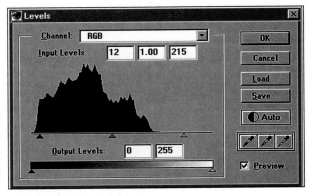

12.3

Using Levels, the black-and-white points are adjusted to 12 and 215 respectively.

A histogram is also displayed in the Levels dialog box (Image, Adjust, Levels or Ctrl+L). You get less information in the Levels dialog box about the histogram, but you can edit the histogram with Levels. In this example, the black point was changed from 0 to 12 and the white point was changed to 215. The output levels were kept at 0 and 255 for the black-and-white points respectively, which caused Photoshop to redistribute all the tones below level 6 (or to the left of the little black triangle) to black and all of the tones above level 215 (or to the right of the small white triangle) to white. In addition, the midtones were redistributed between the two new levels.

12.4

Even with a conservative approach to Levels, the image has much more contrast.

The image on the left is the original image. Notice how the image on the right is more vivid. It has less grays and more contrast, and yet no image detail has been lost. The following are general rules of thumb:

- Reposition the black point to the right of its original position wherever the histogram begins registering dark tones or at the peak of a cluster of dark tones (ideally in the 85–100% black range or 0–50 level range).

- Reposition the white triangle to the left wherever the histogram begins to register light tones or at the peak of a cluster of light tones (ideally in the 15–0% black range or 205–255 level range).

 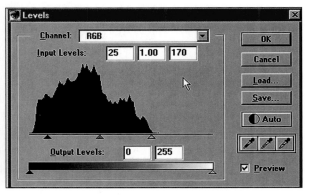

A more radical approach results in even better contrast.

Figure 12.5 was generated with a more radical approach to Levels. By adjusting the black Eyedropper tool to the center of the first peak in the 0–50 level range and the white Eyedropper tool to the beginning of where the brightest levels were, the image is given a much more vivid contrast than the first, more conservative approach.

Unfortunately, it is rare to find or scan an image that won't benefit at least a little from this technique. The black and white Eyedropper tools are rarely properly positioned. Many images, however, don't afford for such extreme manipulation as the one in this example.

Edit color channels to augment the contrast of individual color channels.

INTERFACE DESIGN with Photoshop

Some titles or images on web pages are concentrated in a particular color for effect or because the palette is designed in that color range. In this example, only the Blue channel's levels were edited. The image has a sharper contrast, making the little village scene appear more sad.

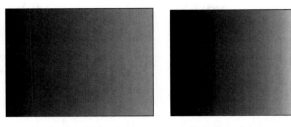

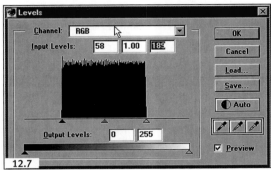

Observe how Levels works on this linear gradient to maximize the contrast and spread out the midtones.

To clarify how the Levels feature works, the gradient to the left in figure 12.7 is from approximately 75% black to approximately 25% black. Adjusting the gradient levels results in the gradient from black to white as shown in the gradient on the right.

Curves

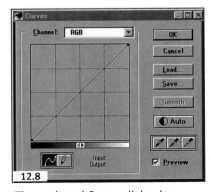

The unaltered Curves dialog box.

Curves (Image, Adjust, Curves, or Ctrl+M) enables you to make more versatile tonal adjustments. Instead of making the adjustments using only three controls, you can adjust any point along the gray-level scale while keeping as many as 15 other points constant. The following discussion gets a bit technical, but it makes working with Curves a little less threatening. With this technical background, you can use Curves to gain complete tonal control over an image.

The vertical axis of the Curves graph maps the original brightness values of the pixels (input levels) and the horizontal axis maps the new brightness values (output levels). Because no pixels have been mapped to new values when the Curves dialog box is initially opened, a diagonal line maps the beginning relationship between the input values and the output values. In RGB mode, by default, the curves are mapped from shadows on the lower left (level 0 or black) to highlights on the upper right (level 255 or white). Curves work opposite for CMYK and grayscale images.

The default graph is in increments of 25%, or 4×4. You can change the grid to increments of 10%, or 10×10, by holding down the Ctrl+Alt keys (Command+Option keys on the Macintosh) and clicking anywhere within the graph with the mouse. Each intersection in a 4×4 grid represent 25% increments from 0%–100%. When you manipulate the 50% point of the graph, you are redistributing the tones in 50% range of the color. All values that are 50% black in an RGB image or a specific channel in an RGB image will be manipulated according to the adjustments made on the graph. Each intersection of a 4×4 grid represents 64 levels (25% of 256) for RGB images.

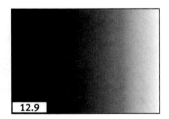

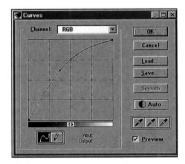

Adjusting the midpoint of the curve to the upper left increases the color (white).

One of the best ways to learn about curves is to observe the results of curve manipulations on a linear gradient from black to white. In fig. 12.9, the center of the curve line has been dragged to the upper left using a single point. Observe how the highlights have been expanded and the shadows have been decreased. Blacks and whites are there, but the midtones have been lightened. Thus, moving a curve to the upper left, in RGB mode, has the effect of increasing the amount of color (in this case white) in that particular range. In RGB color space, white is created by the presence of 100% Red, Green, and Blue.

INTERFACE DESIGN with Photoshop

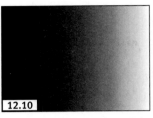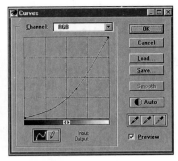

12.10

Adjusting the midpoint of the curve to the lower right decreases the color (white).

With this example, the center of the curve line has been dragged to the lower right using a single point. Observe how the shadows have been expanded and the highlights have been decreased. Again, blacks and whites are still there, but the midtones have been darkened. Thus, moving a curve to the lower right, in RGB mode, has the effect of decreasing the amount of color (in this case white) in that particular range.

This particular manipulation of curves (manipulating the 50% point) is often useful. This adjustment enables you to maintain the position of the 100% and 0% values of a color while manipulating its midtones. You can manipulate the midtones in images that are too dark or too light, for example, while maintaining the black-and-white points. This technique maintains and improves contrast.

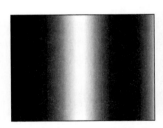

12.11

A more extreme curve manipulation results in a more visible tonal redistribution.

Here is one further example to drive the point home. This curve has been manipulated so that the output values at 50% black are 0% black (level 255) and the output values at 25% black are 100% black (level 0). A point at approximately 75% black (level 64) anchors the shadows from sliding up with the adjustment at the 50% black Eyedropper tool. Notice that the 50% point has been moved up and to the left and the result is more color or 100% white. The inverse is true at the 25% black Eyedropper tool.

It can be educational to try different curve manipulations on a grayscale gradient from black to white to see what the manipulation is doing. When you correlate how the linear gradient image is affected to how RGB images are affected with similar curve operations, you will be well on your way to mastering curves. Now let's move on to how curves can be used to augment an image.

Real-world images are much more random than gradient blends, so we will perform the same manipulations to a grayscale image to observe the results. Each image is different. Some images may have a lot more dark tones than light tones. Curve manipulations must be made in response to the particular characteristics of each image.

A cropped image from KPT Power Photos.

This image from KPT Power Photos has been cropped and has had its levels adjusted. It is dark, with most of the color in the light blues, bright yellows, and oranges. The image is perfectly attractive the way it is, but you can augment certain aspects of the image with Curves if you should so desire.

A midpoint adjustment can increase or decrease the brightness while maintaining the contrast.

INTERFACE DESIGN with Photoshop

If you need to maintain the contrast in the image yet increase the brightness, the 50% point manipulation demonstrated in fig. 12.13 would do the trick. Again, this manipulation has decreased the amount of color density in the midrange, resulting in a brighter image. It's debatable whether this has improved the image or not, but it may be that this sort of operation is needed to make the image more visible on-screen.

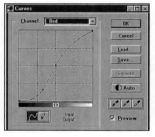

For more control, edit individual channels.

A more involved method of editing an image's curves involves editing individual color channels. In the case of fig. 12.14, oranges and yellows of the sunset were augmented with the red curve and the blues in the water were augmented with the blue curve. Because the reds in this image were mostly concentrated in the shadows, the red curve was augmented only in the 75% tonal range. Most of the blues were in the highlights, so the 25% range of the blue curve was edited. A slight decrease in the highlights on the green provided a little more contrast. Little image degradation has taken place with these tonal manipulations and the image has become much more colorful. See Chapter 2, "RGB Imagery and Palettes," for a discussion on how you can use curves to manipulate tones for optimizing color palettes.

Curve manipulations can be counterintuitive in RGB images. You may have to decrease the density of a color to increase the color in the image.

Decreasing the density of a color in the midtones can have the paradoxical visual effect of bringing out that color more. In fig. 12.15, the blue midtones were decreased, causing the blue shadows to stand out more, especially next to the brighter pixels that the blue midtones were replaced with. This is a good example of how the character of the image dictates the curve manipulation. If you want the blue to really stand out, an argument can be made in the case of this image that the best way to accomplish this is to decrease the overall amount of blue in the image instead of increasing it.

Curves provide an alternative method for adding color casts to an image, as shown with these images from PhotoDisc.

With CMYK images, curves are often used to remove color casts. Often, color casts are used in multimedia and web graphics for visual effect or because they help fit images into a custom palette. A purple color cast has been added to fig. 12.16 from PhotoDisc by increasing the midtones on the blue channel and decreasing the midtones on the red and green channel. Compare this to the original image at the lower left and the same image colorized with the Hue/Saturation feature. Using Curves instead of Colorize provides more depth to an image, while essentially grouping its palette into a specific tonal range.

Selection Techniques

Masking is the backbone of image editing in Photoshop. Masking out images to be used as buttons or for part of a collage is a common task that can be accomplished with masks in Photoshop. Photoshop refers to its masks as selections (designers often use the terms interchangeably). For this discussion we will use the technically accurate designation: "selection." You can store selections in channels. The basic concept behind selections is that you can cover up one part of an image to edit another without worrying about the edits affecting the covered portion. Selections also allow you to cover up a percentage of an image so that only some of the edits or operations affect the selected portion of the image.

One of the nice aspects of working with RGB images (as opposed to high resolution CMYK) is that their lower resolution allows for quicker manipulation and editing of images. Lower resolution also means that detailed work is less of a requirement. Image quality is often further degraded in the process of conforming to a particular palette. People often view so many images in multimedia and on the web that they are not likely to notice when you crop off a few extra pixels or edit stray elements in an image. Although quality should never suffer, it won't hurt most images in multimedia and the web if the selection is less than completely precise. The bottom line is that quick masking techniques are often more than adequate.

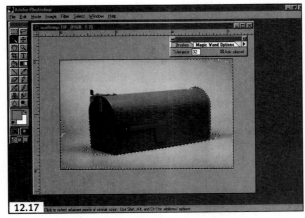

Magic Wand is unable to quickly mask the mailbox.

The mailbox in fig. 12.17 has been cropped from PhotoDisc CMCD. More and more stock objects come with prebuilt selections, but this one does not. The object is to select the mailbox from the background. Two problems exist with doing this: The first is that the shadows are a darker gray than most of the background, and the second is that the mailbox is gray like the majority of the background, which makes it difficult to select the image with the Magic Wand tool. The selection in fig. 12.17, indicated by the dashed line, was generated with the Magic Wand tool using its default setting of 32 Tolerance. The selection does not encompass the entire surroundings of the mailbox and, furthermore, it encompasses some of the top of the mailbox.

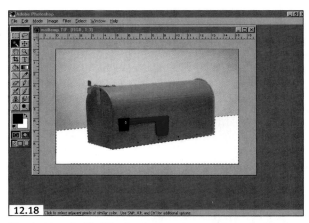

The bottom half of the background was selected with the Lasso tool and deleted.

Sometimes the quickest way to create an accurate selection is to try the Magic Wand tool with various tolerance settings. However, when this doesn't work, you have to get more creative. This strategy for masking the mailbox took advantage of the fact that the mailbox had some straight edges. The bottom half of the background, which contains the shadows, was selected and deleted with the Lasso tool.

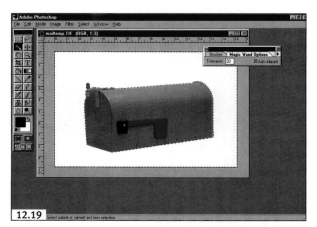

The top half selected and deleted using the Magic Wand.

INTERFACE DESIGN with Photoshop

Now, because the top half of the mailbox has a much more consistent color, it was easy to select by changing the Magic Wand Tolerance to a lower setting (20). After deleting the top half, the Magic Wand tool could be used once more to select the entire background.

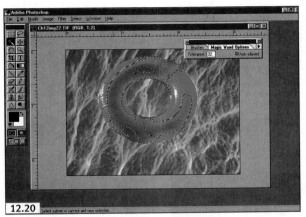

12.20

Selecting the red tube from the background water texture seems to pose a bit of a challenge.

Not all objects have straight edges or gray/white backgrounds. This image, cropped from Kai's Power Photos, makes selection difficult because of the round shape (the tube) and the irregular colors in the background (the water). The screen capture shows how little the Magic Wand captures with the default 32 setting.

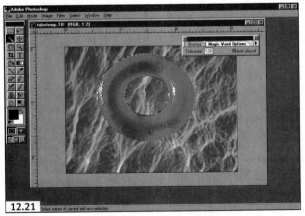

12.21

By increasing the Magic Wand Tolerance, selecting most of the tube becomes easy.

Because the background had such a complete tonal difference from the object, however, nearly all of the object could be selected by adjusting the Tolerance setting for the Magic Wand tool to about 128 (see fig. 12.21). Most of what the Magic Wand has missed—mostly the highlights on the tube—can easily be picked up with the Quick Mask feature.

Although these techniques aren't revolutionary, the point is to look at an image's unique qualities and see if you can take advantage of them to generate quick selections. Rather than spending grueling hours trying to be precise, take advantage of the Feather, Matting, and Modify features to do some of the work for you. In many cases, if a few pixels are shaved off the edges of an image, the audience will never notice.

Button Up and Down States

12.22

Various button up and down states, using images from PhotoDisc, Classic PIO, and CMCD.

Objects and images are excellent candidates for buttons. Images make effective icons as opposed to little pixelated spot illustrations. Common image button down states include reducing the shadow or a glow (see Chapter 6, "Shadows, Glows, and Other Bread and Butter Techniques," for a discussion on these techniques). Another fun possibility is a result-oriented down state. In fig. 12.22, the closed toolbox changes to an open toolbox when the user clicks on it.

Collage and the Non-Static Interface

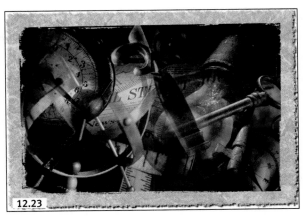

12.23

Collages provide engaging imagery by tastefully mixing a variety of elements.

Collages are effective for backgrounds, as elements for creating visual cohesiveness, and even as interfaces themselves. Often the best backgrounds for a project are those that are creatively mixed together from the subject matter. Collages built with images that are used throughout a project enable users to become a little more consciously or subconsciously familiar with the paradigm. Projects that use consistent placement of images and image icons rather than static frames and static buttons can provide a refreshing change of pace from the more common structured interfaces.

Collages built in Photoshop are mostly a matter of masking the elements and mixing them in creative and tasteful ways. Many chapters in this book cover techniques that can be used to generate unique masks (chapters 8, 9, and 10 are particularly useful for collages). Beyond creative masking techniques, the best tip for creating collages is to take advantage of layer masks.

12.24

Layer masks provide complete versatility for creating collages. The transparency of the object within the collage in this interface—created with images from Image Club and PhotoDisc—can be easily edited by using each layer's layer mask.

In fig. 12.24, each object within the collage (which is built from the objects used for the buttons) has a separate layer mask that controls how the objects blend with one another. Simple gradients are used for this collage, but more complex masks can also be cut and pasted into a layer mask. The advantage of a layer mask over a standard selection is that layer masks keep the entire object intact, instead of deleting portions of the object to achieve the gradient transparency. Layer masks enable you to take a completely different approach without having to rebuild the layer.

A few handy layer mask tips follow:

- ► Use Levels and Curves to make easy and quick modifications to layer masks.

- ► Ctrl/Command-click the layer mask thumbnail to toggle it on and off to preview the layer with or without the layer mask.

- ► Alt/Option-click the layer mask thumbnail toggle on and off to view just the layer mask for editing.

- ► Shift-click the layer mask thumbnail to toggle on and off Quick Mask mode.

- ► Alt/Option-drag the layer mask onto the New Layer icon to create a new channel out of it.

Special Effects

Layers and layer modes provide a wealth of possibilities for special effects with images. By applying various filter effects and then combining them with layer modes, it is easy to add visual interest to scans and other stock imagery and make it difficult to tell they are in fact stock images.

Videoizing

Videoizing an image makes it appear as if it were being viewed on an old television or on a monitor with bad reception.

You can videoize any image, such as this one from PhotoDisc.

1. Create a duplicate layer of the image by dragging down to the layer icon.

2. Apply Mezzotint (Filter, Pixelate) with the Long Strokes option to the duplicate layer.

3. With the duplicate layer still selected, apply the Multiply mode and reduce the opacity to 50–60%.

12.26

The videoized image looks like it's being viewed on an antique television with bad reception, as shown in this example created with images from CMCD and Classic PIO.

Try the other Mezzotint effects as well as the Screen, Overlay, Darken, and Luminosity modes.

Antiqueing

12.27

Even a colorful image such as this one from KPT Power Photos can be made to look antique.

Antiqueing an image makes the image appear to be old and worn. Photos can be made to look old merely by converting them to sepia tone, but roughing the image up a little bit also helps to augment the effect. Antiqueing an image can be a little more involved than videoizing an image.

1. First convert the image to grayscale if it's not grayscale already.

2. Select Duotone from the Mode menu and select Tritone from the Type pop-up menu.

3. Click on the Load button and load the mysepia1.ado from the photoshp\duotones\tritone\process directory (Photoshop/Goodies/Duotone/presets/Tritones/Process/Tritones/BMY Sepia 1 on the Mac). These ado files are optional if you used Photoshop's custom install, so you may have to install them if they are not there.

4. Convert the image back to RGB mode and use Hue/Saturation to increase the saturation of the image about 50–70%.

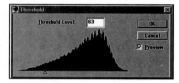

5. Next, select a grainy image such as the one in fig. 12.28 from PhotoDisc. Use Threshhold (Ctrl/Command+T) to isolate some uneven speckles.

6. Crop the image to the same size as the main image, Select all, and Copy.

7. Paste the image as a layer and apply the layer with Multiply or Darken mode. You can reduce the opacity to vary the effect.

Other Interesting Possibilities

The possibilities of dressing up stock images are endless. This section examines ways to create painted effects, sandblasted effects, and lighting effects, and also looks at creating text screens with layers.

Painted Effects

12.30

A painted look with an image from KPT Power Photos.

Many interesting effects can be generated by creating a copy of the original image on another layer, applying effects, and then merging the layers using Layer modes. An artistic painted look can be generated using the following steps:

1. Create a duplicate layer of a photo.

2. Apply a Gaussian Blur (5–7 at 300 dpi, lower at 72 dpi).

3. Merge the layer with its original with the Multiply, Soft Light, Hard Light, and Darken modes.

Sandblasted Effects

A sandblasted look with an image from Corel Professional Photos CD-ROM.

A sandblasted look can be generated using the following steps:

1. Use the High Pass filter with a radius of 25 on a duplicate layer.

2. Apply Threshold using a level almost in the center (126).

3. Merge using the Overlay mode at 30% opacity.

Lighting Effects

Simple lighting effects can be generated with basic gradients.

Unique lighting effects can be achieved by creating a new layer and adding a series of gradients to the layer.

1. Fill a new layer with a diagonal linear gradient from black to white.

2. Generate the multiple gradient bands using the Curves feature with a gyrating curve.

3. Merge the banded gradient with the background using the Darken Mode at 40% opacity.

Reducing Contrast for Text

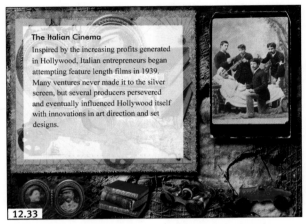

Create text screens with layers instead of altering the main image.

Finally, use layers to create text screens instead of altering the main image.

1. Create a new layer.

2. Fill a selection with white (with the Preserve Transparency option turned off).

3. Set the selection to 85% opacity.

Although some images may be perfect exactly as they are, Photoshop is first and foremost an image editing program. Using the techniques discussed in this chapter, you can tweak and mold an image in just about any way you can imagine. With Photoshop, there's usually no reason why the image can't look just right.

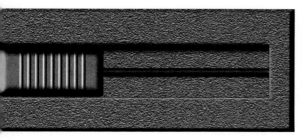

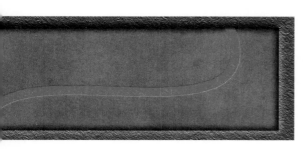

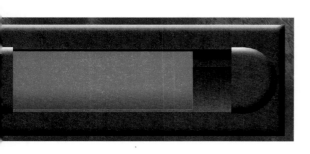

CHAPTER 13

Sliders, Dials, Switches, Doodads, and Widgets

All kinds of gadgets are needed to create interfaces. Effective interfaces are based on real-world objects such as calculators and radio controls. By using gadgets in an interface that are similar to common gadgets in the real world, you can reduce the learning curve substantially. You know how a light switch works or how to read a thermometer. So if you use a switch or meter that looks like a light switch or thermometer, you will often inherently know how to use or read them. Beyond their utility, gadgets and doodads help augment the appeal of many interfaces by serving as interesting visual elements that help fill out the interface.

Covered in this chapter:

► Sliders

► Push Button Switches

► Bar Meters

► Wires

► Screens

► Screws and Nuts

Sliders

Sliders heighten the realism of an interactive interface by providing an element that responds in real time to your direction. You click and hold down on a slider, then drag to the desired position. A classic use for a slider is the volume controls common on both the Macintosh and Windows platforms. You click and drag up or to the right to increase the volume and down or to the left to decrease the volume.

The trick to creating sliders is to integrate them seamlessly over the slider bar. If a slider casts a shadow, it should follow the slider as you drag it, so the shadow is usually part of the slider. Because the shadow is cast on the background, the background needs to be random enough for the shadow to blend in with the background no matter what position it is in. If it's a hard shadow, if the background is a solid color, or if there is no shadow at all, it is easy to integrate the slider seamlessly.

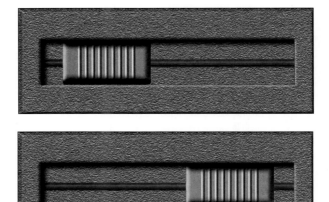

13.1

A slider without a shadow in this case looks unnatural.

This example is a little tricky. Not only does the background have a slight background texture, but the slider slides over a bar. Notice that because the slider is set within a cavity, it looks unnatural without a shadow. You might not consciously notice it, but something about the interface would surely bug you even if you couldn't put your finger on it. This example was created with techniques from Chapters 3, "Textures from Scratch," 4, "The Beveled Look," and 6, "Shadows, Glows, and Other Bread and Butter Techniques."

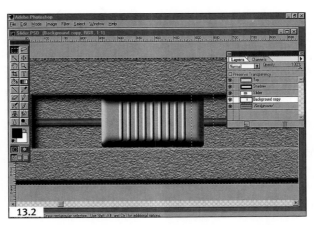

Copy a portion of the background to use for the slider's shadow.

Notice that for this example, there is a top layer with a cutout, a shadow layer of the cutout (see Chapter 6 for details on how to create these effects), a layer for the slider, and a layer for the background. The shadow for the slider that integrates seamlessly with the background as the slider moves can now be created in just a few steps.

1. Make a copy of the background layer by dragging it to the New Layer icon in the lower left corner of the Layers palette.

2. Select an area approximately the same size as existing shadows on the interface. In this example, the shadows on the top and left of the cavity already dictate the visual depth, so make a selection to approximately match those specifications.

3. Invert the selection, delete, and deselect.

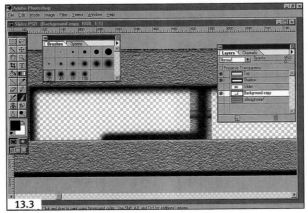

4. Select a brush size that approximately matches the size of the existing shadows, then paint a shadow on the Background copy layer with black.

5. Click the Paintbrush tool at one point, then hold down the Shift key while clicking on another point to draw a straight line between the two points. You can slightly adjust the opacity of the layer afterward to match the shadows. Do not adjust the opacity below 85% or the background will start to show through too much. The previous example shows the Background copy layer with the Background layer turned off so you can see the results of this step more clearly.

6. Ensure that the Background copy layer is below the Slider layer. Turn off all the layers except the Slider and Background copy layers and merge them.

7. Rename the Background copy layer Slider.

You can test how well the slider's shadow integrates with the background by selecting the Slider layer, selecting the Move tool, holding down the Shift key and dragging the slider right and left (or up and down if you've created a vertical slider). Sliders are valuable for controls that have multiple possible settings, but many controls need only two settings: on and off.

Push Button Switches

As previously observed, most people intuitively know how to use switches. Push button switches are similar to button up and down states, except that the down state of a switch remains visible after the switch is clicked. The idea is to create a state or version that looks like the button has been pushed in from its original state.

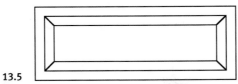

13.5

1. The template for this button was created in CorelDRAW!. Draw a rectangle, then use CorelDRAW!'s Contour feature to create two more rectangles offset .1 inches each inside the original. Use the corners of the two new inner rectangles as guides to draw bevel shapes. Export each bevel shape separately as a template to be used as a channel in Photoshop along with the original and middle rectangles.

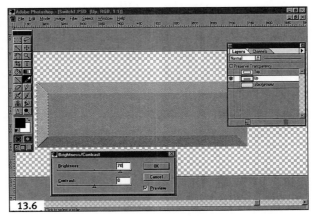

13.6

2. Mask out an area using the middle rectangle from CorelDRAW!, fill it with orange, and apply a monochromatic Noise.

3. Load each bevel as a channel to add brightness values with the Brightness/Contrast filter to achieve the highlights and shadows. Going clockwise from the top side, add Brightness values of 50, −70, −50, and 70 to the bevel selections.

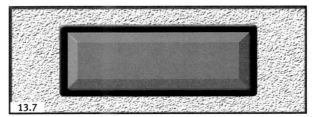

4. Create the top layer (referred to here as "Top" layer) using the Cutout technique demonstrated in Chapter 6. For this state, there is a top layer and a layer for the button (which can be the Background layer but here is referred to as the "Up" layer). This represents the Push Button Switch up state.

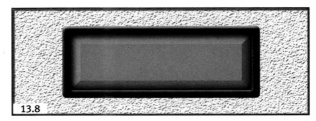

5. To create the down or in state, drag the top layer to the New Layer icon and name it Top Shadow.

6. Drag the Shadow layer below the Top layer, select Fill from the Edit menu, and fill with black with Preserve Transparency selected.

7. With black as the foreground color, load the rectangle used to create the cutout and apply a Stroke (Edit menu) of about 10 pixels.

8. Apply a Gaussian Blur of 5–10 pixels.

9. Create a duplicate of the Up layer, name it Down, and use Brightness/Contrast to apply a –20 Brightness. The Shadow layer should be above the Down layer.

10. To view the results, turn the Shadow and Button In layers on and off to see the in and out or up and down states.

Interactive controls are not the only valuable gadgets used in interface design. Many interfaces require elements that give you information or feedback. These elements are not user-controllable, but rather they are continually updated visual elements that provide you with important information as you progress.

Bar Meters

Bar meters, such as thermometers, are commonly used in multimedia to indicate power levels, lives, temperature, and other information indicators. Bar meters are easy to create with Photoshop, but a little thought must be given to implementing them in multimedia.

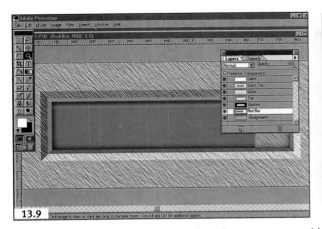

13.9

A meter within an all-encompassing interface poses no problem.

This beveled bar meter, created using the similar techniques discussed previously, uses a separate layer for the red bar. The red bar moves to the left and right to indicate more or less of a given kind of data. In this case, it is easy to move the whole bar right and left because any portion of the bar that moves under the interface is no longer visible.

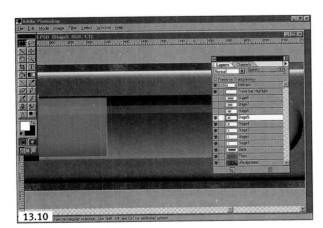

13.10

If the meter is not integrated with a larger interface, you will have to get creative.

Because this example is not integrated with a larger interface, the bar will creep out from behind the endcaps of the meter. To get around this, you must create multiple versions of the meter to represent different stages that are each used separately as the meter goes up or down. You can also take Photoshop out of the loop and just create a simple animation that will play within the meter.

Some elements of interface design add no functionality at all, but rather support the theme or add realism to the theme. Elements such as Wires, Screens, Screws, and Bolts often add no functionality, but elements such as these provide the final touches that allow you to suspend disbelief and become more fully immersed in your virtual world.

Wires

Wires can help augment the feel of an electrical, science fiction, or robotics theme. Here's a quick little wire technique that can be accomplished with the help of a vector-based application.

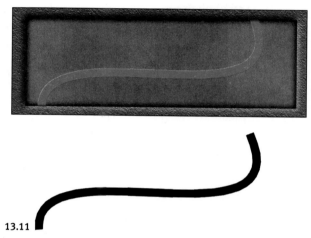

13.11

1. Start by exporting some thick curved lines from a vector-based application. Import each line as a template in Photoshop and create channels out of each one. This discussion assumes that the lines are black and the background is white in each channel. We'll refer to the first line channel as Wire 1. Remember, each line should be exported with a rectangle that is the full size of the interface so the lines are in the correct position when imported in Photoshop.

2. Create a new layer, Select all, delete, load the Wire 1 channel as a selection, invert the selection, and fill it with a color. We'll refer to this layer as Wire 1 layer.

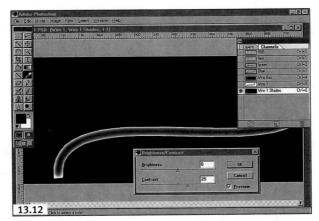

13.12

3. Drag the Wire 1 channel to the New Channel icon in the center of the Channels palette to create a duplicate channel. We'll refer to this channel as Wire 1 Shades.

4. Apply a Gaussian Blur with a 3–5 radius.

5. Load to the Wire 1 Shades channel. Load the Wire 1 channel as a selection and fill with black. Open the Brightness/Contrast dialog box and increase the contrast about 15–25.

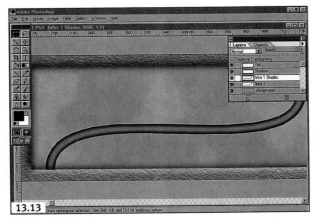

13.13

6. Create a copy of Wire 1 layer and name it Wire 1 Shades. Select all and delete.

7. Load the Wire 1 Shades channel and fill with black. Notice that flaws at the ends of the wire are obscured. This is the basic technique.

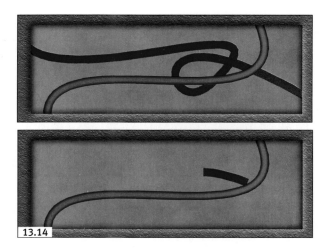

13.14

Creating a wire that loops over itself is not difficult. Follow the basic technique explained previously, then export from your vector application only the portion of the wire that overlaps. This can be used to create a separate series of layers and channels that overlap the main wire. You will have to manually correct or blend out the rounded ends of the shading channel with the Airbrush or Paintbrush tool.

Screens

Screens are used to add intangible flavor to an interface. They can be used to create the look of a small speaker or airduct. Sound or air does not really come out of the elements, but they augment the illusion that the user is working with a real-world interface. This example uses circles, but just about any shape can be used.

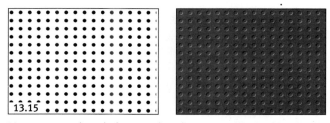

13.15

1. Double-click on the Marquee tool and change the shape to elliptical in the Marquee Options palette.

2. In a blank file, marquee a small perfect circle anywhere on the page by holding down the Shift key while selecting. Fill the selection with black.

3. Change the Shape back to Rectangular in the Marquee Options palette and marquee-select a fairly square area around the circle.

4. Select Define Pattern from the Edit menu and deselect.

5. Select Fill from the Edit menu and fill the file with the pattern.

6. Create a new layer with the dotted pattern, apply a slight Gaussian Blur to the new layer, and a slight Emboss using an angle of approximately −45.

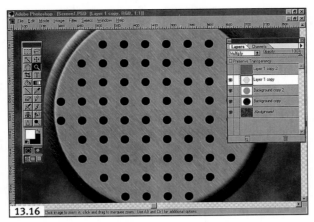

13.16

7. Create an element on which to display the Screen. These circular elements were created with the Quick Emboss technique demonstrated in Chapter 5.

8. Cut and paste the black-and-white dotted pattern into the new file as a layer.

9. Change the mode of the dotted layer to Multiply. If the dots aren't centered over the underlying elements, use the Move tool to nudge the dots into position. Delete any dots that are not fully within the element.

13.17

10. Load the embossed version as a layer.

11. Select the Hard Light mode, then delete the extra embossed dots corresponding to the dots deleted from the black-and-white layer.

12. Merge the layers.

Screws and Nuts

Screws and nuts are often handy to apply the finishing touches to an interface. Screws and nuts can be used to make objects look fastened.

13.18

1. To create a screw, draw a circle with the Elliptical marquee tool and fill with black or import one from a template. Save the circle as a channel.

2. Create a duplicate layer of the circle and apply a Gaussian Blur with a radius of 3–5.

3. Apply an emboss with an angle of approximately 135.

4. Open Levels and use the white Eyedropper tool to click on a 50 percent gray area. Name this layer Shadow.

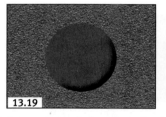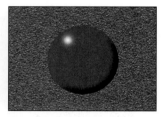

13.19

5. Use the Circle mask to create a circle over a background. Fill the circle with medium gray or any other color you prefer.

6. Apply the Shadows layer with the Multiply mode and merge.

7. Change the Foreground color to white, double-click on the Paintbrush tool, and select a fairly large brush.

8. Click in the upper left region of the circular area to create a highlight. Incidentally, this is an easy way to create a simple little ball.

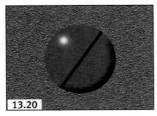 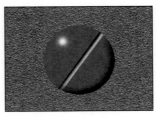

9. Load the Circle channel and use it to draw two diagonal lines, one black and one white. Draw the black line first and then the white line slightly down and the right of the black line. Try to overlap the lines slightly.

10. Begin with a six-sided polygon and a small circle created from a vector-based application. Load each as a separate layer and channel.

 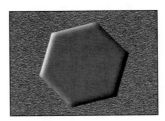

11. Create a new layer, Select all, delete, and deselect. Load the Polygon channel and fill with medium gray. Create a new layer, fill with white and use the Polygon channel to fill the polygon shape with black. Use the Quick Emboss technique discussed in Chapter 5 to emboss the polygon.

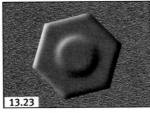 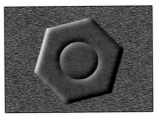

12. Use the Quick Emboss technique to emboss the inner circle layer, then load the Circle channel and Invert (Image, Map).

Adding these small elements to an interface helps add realism and depth. Non-functional touches that complete the theme of the interface can help the user get immersed in the virtual world you are creating. Avoid adding too many intangible elements. Excessive stylistic elements can backfire and result in a distracting interface.

PART III

Extras

Photoshop Tips

This appendix covers some Photoshop tips that will help you increase your effiency and productivity. These tips are in addition to the numerous tricks and time-saving advice found throughout the book.

Layers

Photoshop's layers are a godsend to interface design production. One of the best tips for using Photoshop for interface design is to make full use of layers by placing and creating elements on different layers. Even highlights and shadows should be created on separate layers from the objects they appear to be on whenever possible. Elements that do not overlap can be grouped on the same layer to keep from having to scroll excessively on the Layers palette. By using plenty of layers, you ensure that the interface is as editable as possible. Also, interface design elements can more easily be repurposed when they are on separate layers.

Zoom

Hold down the Ctrl+Alt+"+"/Command+Option+"+" keys to zoom to 16:1. Hold down the Ctrl+Alt+"−"/Command+Option+"−" keys to zoom to 1:16. Double-click on the Zoom tool to zoom to 1:1. Also, to access zoom functions while working with another tool, hold down Ctrl+"+"/Command+"+" to zoom in and Ctrl+"−"/Command+"−" to zoom out or Ctrl+spacebar/Command+spacebar to temporarily access the Zoom In tool and Ctrl+Alt+spacebar/Command +Option+spacebar to temporarily access the Zoom Out tool. Hold down the spacebar to temporarily access the Grabber Hand tool.

Avoid Reinventing the Wheel

Rather than re-creating common interface elements or layers and channels used to create common elements every time you need them, save them to a library file or a series of library files. Keep in mind that it is very easy to repurpose interface design elements with Photoshop without being overly obvious by changing subtle characteristics such as size, color, or orientation. Finally, save often—probably the most important tip of all.

Plug-Ins

Netscape Navigator and Microsoft Explorer both support plug-ins that can be used to deliver multimedia over the web. After plug-ins are installed, they can expand the browser's capability to understand new MIME (Multipurpose Internet Mail Extensions) types. MIME is an Internet standard for delivering non-text–based content such as audio, video, and animations.

When a file that uses a particular MIME type is encountered, the browser passes the information to the plug-in for playback. Along with specialized applications such as CGI programs and Java applications as well as the up-and-coming ActiveX technology, plug-ins can help transform dry web pages into engaging multimedia sites.

At the time of this writing, several plug-ins exist for delivering multimedia over the web. Shockwave for Director is currently among the leading plug-ins for delivering multimedia over the web. Shockwave allows for delivery of multimedia over the Internet in effectively the same fashion as CD-ROM and Kiosk-based multimedia. The main limitation is the time it takes to download a Shockwave file. CD-ROM and Kiosk-based multimedia Director files can be upward of several dozen megs and more; thus, Shockwave files deliver minimal content and must be compressed. Macromedia provides Afterburner, a compression program that compresses Shockwave files for quicker delivery over the Internet. Several strategies exist for creating

Shockwave files that are small, yet deliver visually appealing content that include using multiple instances of the same cast member and using 4-bit images.

Several other plug-ins are available for delivering multimedia over the Internet. The Astound Web Player delivers Astound multimedia files over the Internet. Adobe Acrobat 3.0 provides rudimentary multimedia. Many more similar technologies are in the works for delivering multimedia over the web. However, until broader band lines—such as cable, T1, and ISDN—become more common, these Internet technologies for delivering multimedia over the web require designers to be very creative in order to create engaging content that downloads quickly enough for users to stay interested.

Users are required to download and load the plug-ins. This alone can be a deterrent for some people. It's important to make it as easy as possible for people to acquire the plug-in or plug-ins you are using by providing links to the download sites. In the future, some of the plug-ins, such as Shockwave, will be built directly into the browser.

GALLERY OF REAL-WORLD IMAGES

This book presented you with various techniques for creating elements for your interface. These techniques were designed to help you put the elements together in an effective, creative manner. This gallery depicts interfaces designed by top graphic artists who used techniques like those presented in this book. Browse through and let their creativity spark your own.

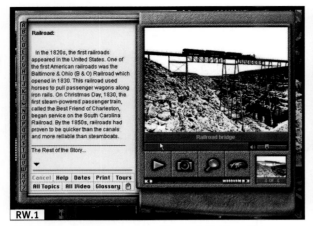

Media Player from Discovery Channel Multimedia's "Skytrip America" by Kyle Anderson.

Weather Database from Discovery Channel Multimedia's "Operation: Weather Disaster" by Kyle Anderson.

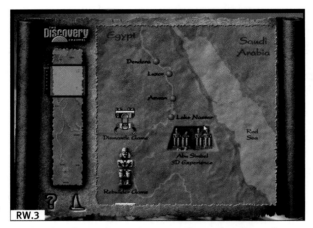

Navigational Map from Discovery Channel Multimedia's "Nile: Passage to Egypt" by Kyle Anderson.

Kyle Anderson, art director at Human Code, begins the interface design process by roughing out his design with sketches. After Kyle decides on a design, he scans his sketches and uses them as templates in Photoshop. Kyle likes to keep his use of colors to a few chosen groups to help focus the interface. For example, on the Media Player interface from Discovery Channel Multimedia's "Skytrip America," Kyle used two main color groups—brown and green—to help group and focus the interface. By using fewer colors, the user is able to focus more on the content and less on the interface. Kyle prefers to work out the functional aspects of the interface and then add stylistic elements. Kyle added the stylized electronic background to the Weather Database from Discovery Channel Multimedia's "Operation: Weather Disaster" only after completing the main elements of the interface. Human Code has become known for innovative approaches to interface design. A great example of their resourcefulness can be found on the Navigational Map interface on Discovery Channel Multimedia's "Nile: Passage to Egypt." To display the long map that the users would be traveling on, Kyle created a small version of a map with a slider that accesses a bird's eye view of the map on the larger screen to the right.

INTERFACE DESIGN with Photoshop

Project Portfolio for GSD&M Advertising by Chipp Walters,
President and CEO of Human Code.

Chipp Walters used a combination of the chrome technique and effective use of color and texture to create this engaging interface for GSD&M Advertising's Project Portfolio. Chipp designed the interface to feature a generous viewing screen while still maintaining access to all the important elements of interface. Chipp used rich browns with a subtle texture to help bring out the colors of the GSD&M logo and provide a basis of contrast to the chrome effect.

Promotional Demo Interface for CDFactory by David Avila.

David Avila, Interface Designer at Human Code, utilizes sketches and templates from Adobe Illustrator to build his interfaces. David is a firm believer in using plenty of layers, and typically his interfaces are comprised of dozens of layers. David likes to avoid using solid white and black for his highlights and shadows. David also resists applying textures to every interface. On the promotional Demo Interface for Human Code's CDFactory technology, David used rich solid colors to aid the gameboard theme and go with the cartoon-esque narrator.

Internezzo Café Demo, Design: Gordon Kio and Brad Johnson, Brad Johnson Presents.

Virtual Antarctic Bridge, Design: Brad Johnson, Brad Johnson Presents. Photo inlay: Jonathan Chester, Extreme Images.

Brad Johnson created the basic demo interface for Internezzo Café in Photoshop. Brad then used texture maps and bump maps to create pizza toppings within Strata Studio Pro. Next, he adjusted the levels and curves of each rendering from Strata Studio Pro. Mountain Travel•Sobek and World Travel Partners wanted Brad to create an interface that was highly updatable for their Virtual Antarctic Bridge project (www.terraquest.com/va/bridge/bridge.html). Brad generated separate GIFs in Photoshop for each data field on the interface so that the data could be updated from Antarctica up to eight times a day. Furthermore, Brad created multiple GIFs for the thermometers so that they could be updated as well. Finally, Brad kept a Photoshop file with the prebuilt highlights and shadows for the image that displays in the middle of the interface. Jonathan Chester relayed an image to Brad which he then used in the prebuilt Photoshop file to update the central image on a daily basis.

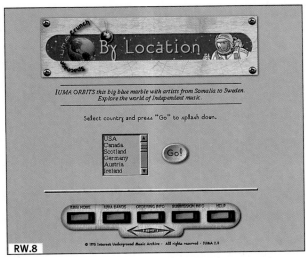

By Location interface for Internet Underground Music Archive's web site by Brandee Selck.

Extras interface for Internet Underground Music Archive's web site by Brandee Selck.

Brandee used scans from a series of '50s era items to create the interfaces for the Internet Underground Music Archive's (IUMA) web site (www.iuma.com). Brandee used the back of an old clothes iron as the background for the By Location page. Brandee blurred a scan from some old wallpaper for the Cool Extras page. According to creative director, Danny Johnson, the IUMA web site attempts to capture the sense of fascination with new technology that was prevalent in the '50s by using retro scans and themes.

TheWowFactor interface by Tom Messina, Mike Cadunzi, and Frank Wanicka.

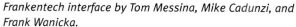

Frankentech interface by Tom Messina, Mike Cadunzi, and Frank Wanicka.

The creative members of Total Concept approach interface design as a team. Frank Wanicka begins by sketching the interfaces. Mike Cadunzi then scans the sketches and builds templates inside Adobe Illlustrator. After this is done, Mike uses the templates to generate the interfaces with Photoshop. Tom Messina then intergrates them onto the web. Mike uses Photoshop's layer modes to create many of his effects. For instance, the chrome bars behind the main interface on TheWowFactor interface were created by combining three different versions of the bars with layer modes. Total Concept prefers to create everything from scratch to avoid looking like other web sites.

Buttons interface for Screen Caffeine Pro by Rick Ligas, Jawai Interactive, Inc.

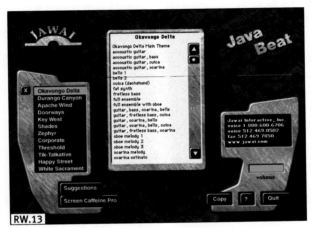

Java Beat interface by Rick Ligas, Jawai Interactive, Inc.

Rick Ligas is so fond of using original textures for Jawai Interactive, Inc.'s interfaces that he created a product out of textures he generated from scratch: Screen Caffeine Pro. The interfaces shown in figs. RW.13 and RW.14 were both created using textures that Rick generated from scratch in Photoshop. Jawai Interactive, Inc., strives to generate interfaces that have all of the controls and content on one screen. "Users should always know where they are and what is available to them," explains Rick. Jawai Interactive, Inc., also prefers for their interfaces to provide plenty of user feedback and forgiveness. Buttons looked depressed when users click on them so that users know something is happening and can roll off the buttons if they don't actually want to click them.

Shoot Video Like A Pro interface by Maria Marchetti, Red Hill Studios, concept by Bob Hone.

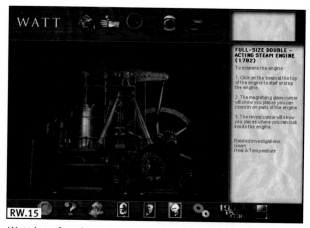

Watt interface by Todd Reamon of Red Hill Studios, 3D by Mike Lucas of Foundry Animation, concept by Bob Hone, published by Houghton Mifflin Interactive.

Red Hill Studios prefers to adhere to real-world metaphors whenever possible. Red Hill Studios believes that interfaces that emulate real-world metaphors should operate within real-world limitations. For example, buttons should not disappear or be magically repositioned. For the Shoot Video Like A Pro interface, Maria Marchetti composited scans from remote controls, cell phones, speakers, and other gadgets to generate an interface reminiscent of a typical camcorder panel. The metaphor thus takes advantage of the real-world metaphor that the user is employing in conjunction with the title. Todd Reamon used Photoshop to generate textures and correct the gamma on the 3D renderings for the Watt interface. When interfaces are not tied to real-world metaphors, as in the case of the Watt interface, Red Hill Studios allows for more liberty with button functionality. For example, buttons can disappear when not needed or be replaced with another function when appropriate.

*Dive Guanaja Internet/CD-ROM Prototype interface by
Nancy Tweddell, Graphic Impressions.*

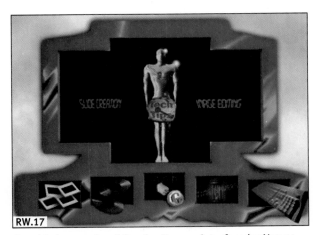

*Graphic Impressions' Service Bureau interface by Nancy
Tweddell, Graphic Impressions.*

Nancy Tweddell likes to use colorful graphic design that draws attention to her web interfaces. Nancy stresses eye-catching interface design as opposed to elaborate functionality because she feels that the most important thing is for users to get involved in the site or title. She likes to minimize the possibility that users will get frustrated and give up on the site. Nancy used Kai's Power Tools and Adobe Gallery Effects in addition to Photoshop's filters to generate her texture, although she prefers to tweak them heavily rather than rely on the initial effects from filters. Nancy builds her textures using layers and layer blending modes to gain more flexibility and control.

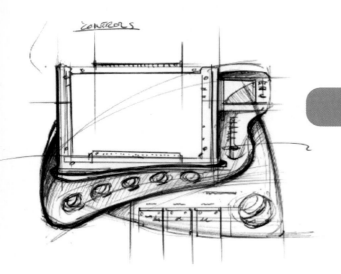

Index

e!

New Riders has emerged as a premier publisher of computer books for the professional computer user. Focusing on CAD/graphics/multimedia, communications/internetworking, and networking/operating systems, New Riders continues to provide expert advice on high-end topics and software.

Check out the online version of *New Riders' Official World Wide Yellow Pages, 1996 Edition* for the most engaging, entertaining, and informative sites on the Web! You can even add your own site!

Brave our site for the finest collection of CAD and 3D imagery produced today. Professionals from all over the world contribute to our gallery, which features new designs every month.

From Novell to Microsoft, New Riders publishes the training guides you need to attain your certification. Visit our site and try your hand at the CNE Endeavor, a test engine created by VFX Technologies, Inc. that enables you to measure what you know—and what you don't!

http://www.mcp.com/newriders

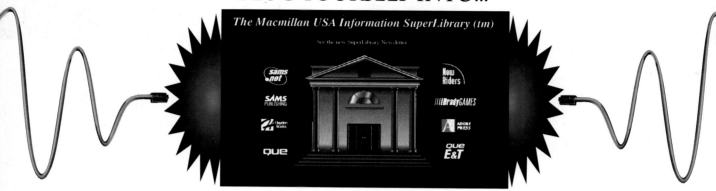

REGISTRATION CARD

Interface Design with Photoshop

Name _____ Title _____

Company _____ Type of business _____

Address _____

City/State/ZIP _____

Have you used these types of books before? ☐ yes ☐ no

If yes, which ones? _____

_____

How many computer books do you purchase each year? ☐ 1–5 ☐ 6 or more

How did you learn about this book? _____

Where did you purchase this book? _____

Which applications do you currently use? _____

_____

Which computer magazines do you subscribe to? _____

_____

What trade shows do you attend? _____

_____

Comments: _____

_____

_____

Would you like to be placed on our preferred mailing list? ☐ yes ☐ no

☐ **I would like to see my name in print!** You may use my name and quote me in future New Riders products and promotions. My daytime phone number is: _____

New Riders Publishing   201 West 103rd Street ◆ Indianapolis, Indiana 46290 USA

Fax to **317-581-4670**

Fold Here

- -